*Unlocking the
Secret World*

Unlocking

the

Secret

World

A Unique
Christian
Ministry
to Abused,
Abandoned,
and
Neglected
Children

Wayne & Diane Tesch

Tyndale House Publishers, Inc.
WHEATON, ILLINOIS

Library of Congress Cataloging-in-Publication Data

Tesch, Wayne.
    Unlocking the secret world : a unique Christian ministry to abused, abandoned, and neglected children / by Wayne and Diane Tesch.
        p.   cm.
    ISBN 0-8423-7735-2 : $9.99
    1. Sexually abused children—Pastoral counseling of.   2. Sexually abused children—Case studies.   3. Sexually abused children—Rehabilitation.   4. Royal Family Kids' Camps, Inc. I. Tesch, Diane.   II. Title.
BV4464.3.T47   1995
259'.08'6945—dc20   94-45046
                                                                                                                            CIP

Printed in the United States of America

00   99   98   97   96   95
7   6   5   4   3   2   1

We dedicate this book to the children who have been forced to live their nightmares in secret. We hope they can now unlock their hearts and gain hope for a better life.

CONTENTS

ACKNOWLEDGMENTS

Many people have influenced the development of Royal Family Kids' Camps, Inc., and of this book.

We thank our parents, who have prayed for us and have done our daily tasks to move us along in "growing a dream."

We thank our daughter and son-in-law, Renee and Paul. Thank you, Renee, for seeing our struggles and rejoicing with us at every milestone. Thank you, Paul, for praying for us and for taking Renee as your wife, completing a cycle in her life and giving us freedom as her parents to concentrate on ministry. Your home has been a respite for us in nurturing the dream.

We thank Dr. George O. Wood. George, when I was your senior associate pastor, you gave us the freedom to try a new idea like Royal Family and moved us beyond despair by sharing the starfish story. Your many sermons are a foundation for this book.

We thank the four angels—you know who you are—for whom Vicki Barnes prayed on that Friday evening in our home. You have lifted us to new heights and helped us soar beyond adversity.

We thank Wendell Hawley for taking a chance on new authors and Lynn Vanderzalm for making this a peak experience for us. You've made book publication one of the easier accomplishments in our lives.

We thank Dale Berkey and the staff at Berkey Brendel Sheline for pulling together and making our dream a reality.

We thank Johanna Townsend and Renee Davis for your sensitivity and creativity in bringing God's Word to a level that abused children grasp and understand. Your work also has helped them unlock the secret world.

We thank our Newport-Mesa Christian Center friends, who believed in the Royal Family idea and launched us into a full-time ministry. Your support is invaluable.

We thank Gary and Lila Morris at the Green Heron Nursery & Espresso in Poulsbo, Washington. Under your gazebo we gained inspiration for this book.

We thank the camp directors, for without your untiring dedication and commitment, the dream of Royal Family Kids' Camps, Inc., would still be just that—a dream. You have given that dream flesh and bones and have made it breathe life into desperate children.

Finally, we thank the camp counselors and staff members. You are the hands and arms that heal, don't hurt, precious children.

PART ONE

A Unique Christian Ministry to Abused, Abandoned, and Neglected Children

Entering the Secret World

This book should never have been written. The very existence of child abuse and neglect in America is anathema to everything decent and human in our society. It would be better if we already had solved this problem and if this book were merely a record of the history of child abuse and neglect. That, of course, is not the case, which makes this book all the more pertinent.

From the first line of chapter 1, in which my friends Wayne and Diane Tesch tell us about a boy named Shorty, to the last paragraph of the book, which challenges us to be willing to work hard to help broken and battered children, I found myself looking into a mirror.

Although I am sixty years old, I was a Shorty. Instead of packing all my worldly possessions in a paper grocery sack, I packed them into two cardboard boxes secured from our corner grocery store. I was a seven-year-old Franky, like the boy in this book: Although my parents sent me to Sunday school, I was sexually abused at home. I was like the child who had so few clothes that she had to improvise the wearing and washing of her two pairs of underwear just to make it through the week at camp.

The names of the kids whose stories are recounted in this book are not their real names. But in reading the book, please understand that they are *real* children and these are their *real* experiences. Changing their names does not make this a work of fiction.

My own experiences of neglect and abuse definitely were part of a secret world; no one talked about child abuse then. But while I couldn't talk to anyone about what was happening to me, I did find help in the form of loving Christian adults. My first day in Sunday school at age five was the first time I remember being hugged and told that I was loved. Mrs. Miller was my first Sunday school teacher and my first mentor. I also went to camp when I was seven years old. It was not Royal Family Kids' Camps, but it was the 1940s equivalent. I don't remember the name of my counselor, but he was a one-week mentor of extraordinary importance to me. For three of my preteen years Annie Dahlberg was my mentor. She kept me busy in Sunday school and church and kept hope alive within me. And in my early teen years Don and Mary Lee Lang gave me strong spiritual and moral support.

Child abuse is destroying lives today. As statistics in the following chapters will reveal, over 3 million cases of child abuse and neglect were reported in America in 1993. All these children need someone to learn about their condition, someone willing to do something to help them in their despair. They need hugs, people to talk to, people who give them encouragement and a real sense of self-esteem. Most important, these children need to know that they are wanted and loved.

Can just one week at Royal Family Kids' Camps make a difference? Absolutely yes! One week at camp did it for me when I was seven years old. It forever changed my life.

I have met some of the Royal Family Kids' Camps counselors and have seen their compassion, their dedication, and their resolve to help abused children. I've seen their tears. I've seen their excitement at little changes in just one child. And I've seen their sacrifices in giving themselves to help others.

Part 1 of this book will introduce you to the problem of child abuse through both statistics and the stories of real children. As you meet these children, open your heart to them. Let them motivate you to involve yourself, your family, your friends, and your church in the secret world of abused and neglected children.

Part 2 explores in greater detail the impact of child abuse on children, the family, and the church. Several chapters give clear steps that can help you and your church make a difference in the lives of children nobody seems to love.

DR. DONALD K. C. NORTH
President, Donor Non-Profit Counselling, Inc.

CHAPTER ONE

Child Abuse: An Epidemic

Shorty came to camp with all his possessions packed in a paper grocery sack. Although camp lasted only a week, Shorty had brought with him everything he owned. He knew that after camp he would be leaving with a different foster family, not the family that had dropped him off. He was seven years old, moving into his tenth foster home. In his paper bag he had no baby album, no birthday-party snapshots, no baseball-card collection—just a few clothes.

As the camp bus made its way down the mountainside, taking Shorty to his new family and his new foster home, he sat next to us on the bus, his L.A. Dodger baseball cap cocked to one side. He didn't know where he was headed, and we didn't have any assurances for him. But because of his week with us at camp, he knew that God loved him and would be with him.

Shorty is one of millions of abused and neglected children

in our nation. While some of these kids are removed from their homes, others are left in their abusive families; no one knows which is worse. It's a national tragedy that this year about 3 million children will be reported as abused or neglected, and thousands of other cases of abuse or neglect will go unreported.

Shorty and children like him live in a secret world, a world in which children dream about monsters that perform horrendous deeds on their bodies but then awaken to the reality that their monsters are *real*. The secret world is full of children who are locked in closets, thrown against walls, pummeled with fists or belts, and told, "I wish you were never born!" The secret world is crowded with children who tiptoe in their own home or apartment, awaiting the next explosion that launches them once again into the cycle of abuse.

Child abuse is no secret to the abusers or the victims. But to society it is a secret kept. It is a secret kept from those of us who are not aware of the devastating effects of child abuse, abandonment, or neglect.

We write this book in hopes of unlocking that secret world. For children paralyzed with fear, this book provides a key to unlock their world of abuse and to bring them hope. For adult Christians, this book provides the key to meaningful action that will allow them to be the arms and legs and voice of hope to abused children.

When a doctor faces a fast-spreading illness, that doctor can choose to try to fight back the illness alone or choose to awaken other medical professionals to help stop the epidemic. This book sounds a wake-up call to the Christian church to join forces and work together to stop the epidemic of child abuse in America.

God has always loved children, but mankind has not always shared that love for children. History shows that at different times and in different cultures, children have been used, abused, sacrificed to idols, treated like property, and treated worse than animals. It was the eighteenth century before the philosopher Rousseau finally awakened the idea that children were humans rather than property when he wrote, "Let us speak less of the duties of children and more of their rights."

What are children's rights? If we could make a Bill of Rights for Children, we would say that children should have the right

- to life
- to be received with joy
- to a gentle upbringing
- to find their unique identity
- to walk with God

These rights won't ever be legislated. They won't even be widely accepted. The one that is doubtless accepted by every thinking American adult is the right to a gentle upbringing: Children should never learn violence, hatred, fear, or ridicule at the hands of their caretakers. But even this right is not guaranteed to all children in today's society. Our experience with the abused and neglected children has inspired us to write this book, to let Christians see what is being perpetrated on America's children, and to challenge them to do something about it. Christians clothed in God's love are the best hope for abused children, children whom we have met and have learned to love, children whom you will meet in the pages of this book. Children like Shorty.

God called us to create a summer camp for kids like Shorty, children who have been removed from their homes because of child abuse or neglect, children who desperately need to know the father-love of God and the family-love of Christian adults who would never hurt them. But since God planted that seed in our lives, we have heard repeatedly how important it is to reach out to abused children. We hear this not from the children, who wouldn't necessarily know how to say it, but from adults we meet on the street, in the mall, or at the barbershop. The fact that the frequency and severity of child abuse has remained a secret is incredible, because when we are willing to listen, people everywhere have a story of abuse to tell.

- In Illinois we had shared in a missions conference about the problems of child abuse. Following the service, a young woman sought us out and said, "I'm glad you talked about child abuse tonight. You shared a statistic—that 80 percent of the prostitutes walking the streets of America today were sexually victimized as young girls. You're from Southern California. I used to 'work the streets' between First and Fourth Streets on Harbor Boulevard in Santa Ana. Somehow God came into my life and saved me from all of that. Now I live here; I have a husband and two children who love me. But I really could have used a camp like yours when I was a child."
- In Sacramento, California, we were shopping when a

saleswoman asked if we were visiting the area. When we told her we were in town to tape a television news interview about our ministry, the woman began to share her story. "I was raised by my father. My mother abused me and my brother, but the courts wouldn't believe my father and refused to move us into his custody. Finally my grandmother gave him Polaroid pictures that showed wounds all across my back from a beating my mom had given me with an electric cord when I was four. I don't remember most of what my mom did to me, but I do remember her making my brother stand in the corner of the room while she knocked his head into the corner to discipline him. She did this a lot."

- Waiting at the barbershop, a friend of the barber sat and had coffee and donuts with us. "I think what you're doing is really needed," he began, and we could tell a story was on the way. "My dad beat us. As we got older, his abuse got worse. I think he was hardest on me because I am the oldest. I remember one day when I was a freshman in high school. He beat me so hard that he knocked my top teeth backward, broke my jaw, and gave me a black eye."

- In Minneapolis, Minnesota, after a chapel service at North Central Bible College, a young woman approached with tears running down her face. She said, "Thank you for sharing about child abuse this morning. I was one of those young girls you talked about. But I want you to know, these tears are not tears of sorrow. These are tears of joy, that *finally* someone is talking about child abuse the way it is."

- When we went to open a bank account, the new-account representative, a woman named Carla, asked if we could help her son.[1] Her story was heartrending. Carla's husband had been a violent alcoholic who abused both her and their children. Before he had committed suicide, he had cold-bloodedly murdered their nine-year-old son, then shot and wounded the seven-year-old and three-year-old boys. It was the youngest one, Carey, whom she hoped we could help. Since his father's death, Carey, now eight years old, had turned morose and melancholy. He suffered horrible nightmares. He still wet the bed.

It's shocking that so many total strangers share their stories of child abuse with us just because we are willing to listen. But the statistics prove that child abuse and neglect are more prevalent than we would like to think. About one in four adult women and one in six adult men were abused as children. Of your four best female friends, one was probably an abused child. Of the best six male members of your church choir, one was probably an abused child.

In fact, you may have been abused as a child. This isn't a book to tell you how to deal with those memories, but if you are still haunted by that abusive past, let us quickly share something that you absolutely must believe: What happened to you wasn't your fault, and you mustn't blame yourself. Child abuse, including child sexual abuse, is perpetrated by sick adults, and you were in no way responsible. When you were a child, you had no control over the situation. You could have done nothing to prevent it. Don't blame yourself. That is a mistake. If you are still troubled by what happened to you, talk to your pastor or a Christian counselor. Your past doesn't have to haunt you. It's over, and you can live a victorious life.

Child Abuse: Today and Yesterday

Child abuse today is not as secret as it has been in the past, as evidenced in these statistics provided by the National Committee for the Prevention of Child Abuse and the U.S. Department of Justice.

- In 1993 about 3 million cases of child abuse or neglect were reported.
- Children ages five and under account for 43 percent of all reported child-abuse cases.
- Between 75 percent and 90 percent of reported physical abuse and neglect cases involve the caretakers of the abused children.

The same sources show that the correlation between abuse as a child and the potential for juvenile or adult criminal behavior is also appalling:

- In one study, every death-row inmate in San Quentin reported growing up in a violent, abusive environment.[2]
- Ninety-seven percent of hard-core juvenile delinquents report a history of severe physical punishment and even assault in the home.
- Eighty percent of all prostitutes report sexual abuse as children.

Although these statistics are daunting, do they mean that

child abuse is worse today than it ever was in the past? We don't really think so. It's just that society is just beginning to unlock the secret world of child abuse.

Historically, it has been legal to sell one's children, as was codified as far back as 1792 B.C. by Hammurabi, the ancient Babylonian lawgiver.[3] In 700 B.C. the law called Patria Protestar gave a father the right to sell, mutilate, or even kill his offspring.[4] In Old Testament times, it was a man's right to treat his children as property.

When Abraham's nephew Lot took two strangers into his home, the men of his city, Sodom, surrounded the house, demanding that he surrender his two guests. Instead, Lot offered the men his two daughters. "Let me bring them out to you, and you can do what you like with them," Lot says to the mob (Gen. 19:8). Lot's guests were actually angels of God. They rescued Lot and his daughters from the men of Sodom, but Lot was willing to bargain with the very lives of his children.

The Greek philosopher Aristotle reflected the opinion of his time when he wrote, "The justice of a master or father is different from that of a citizen, for a son or slave is property, and there can be no injustice to one's own property." In ancient Greece the practice of pederasty allowed an adult male legally to court the affections of a boy twelve years old or older. If the arrangement was acceptable to the boy's father, the boy would exchange sexual favors with the suitor in return for training, military equipment, and other gifts. What we would consider to be child abuse today was commonplace in Greek society.[5]

All this is not to say that because child abuse was commonplace it was ever right or considered lightly in the eternal scheme of things. The human sacrifice of babies to the god Molech was despicable in the eyes of Jehovah, the God who rescued little Ishmael from starvation in the wilderness, young Isaac from sacrifice on the altar, and baby Moses from death at the hands of the Egyptians. It was the Lord Jesus who called a little child to himself and told his disciples, "Unless you are converted and become as little children, you will by no means enter the kingdom of heaven. . . . Whoever receives one little child like this in My name receives Me. Whoever causes one of these little ones who believe in Me to sin, it would be better for him if a millstone were hung around his neck, and he were drowned in the depth of the sea" (Matt. 18:3-6, NKJV).

In fact, Christ gave special significance to children, saying, "See that you do not look down on one of these little ones. For I tell you that their angels in heaven always see the face of my Father in heaven" (Matt. 18:10).

Like so many of the best ideas of Christianity, the idea that children are cherished by God and ought to be cherished by adults has not blossomed easily. During the Industrial Revolution, children legally worked in coal mines, lumber mills, factories—places that we would not think of sending a child. These children were sentenced to work long, grueling days. It was during the Industrial Revolution that child abuse was finally recognized, all because of a young girl named Mary Ellen.

Mary Ellen: The First Case Study

Mary Ellen lived with her adoptive parents, but it wasn't much of a life. She was chained to her bed, fed only bread and water, and often ill. A church worker who was visiting an elderly woman in Mary Ellen's tenement learned of the young girl's plight and decided to do something to help her.

When church workers and nurse Etta Wheeler came to Mary Ellen's home, they found her badly beaten body still chained to the bedpost. She was barely alive. But local authorities told the church workers they could do nothing because no law on the books prevented a parent from treating a child any way the parent pleased. Out of desperation, the church turned to Henry Bergh, the founding spirit behind the American Society for the Prevention of Cruelty to Animals. Would *he* help Mary Ellen? After all, she was a part of the animal kingdom.

The ASPCA came to the rescue and removed the young girl as if she were an abused animal. They brought the parents to court for the crime of abuse. Mary Ellen was carried into court on a stretcher, her emaciated and battered body showing the evidence of vicious treatment. Mary Ellen was removed from the parents' custody, and they were given a term in a penitentiary.[6]

People of that day were shocked to realize that the question of cruelty to animals had been regarded as more important than the question of cruelty to children. As a result, the battle for child protection was first taken on by a society for the protection of animals—because that is how children had been regarded in society.

It is interesting to note that it was church workers who discovered Mary Ellen's plight and fought for her well-being. Down through history, the Christian church has tried to cope with the business of child protection. In the 1600s the church established the "poor laws," one of which stated that if a family could not economically provide for their children, the church overseers had the right to remove those children from the home and place them in better circumstances.

This, then, is the historical perspective of child abuse:

- It is an age-old problem.
- It had not been recognized as abuse until the nineteenth century and the case of Mary Ellen.
- Certain people and the church have always tried to do away with child abuse and act as a light in this dark part of society.
- Eventually America incorporated laws to protect abused and neglected children, most of whom were removed from their homes and placed in civil institutions rather than with volunteer agencies.

Yet in spite of the laws, every four hours a child dies from abuse or neglect in our society.[7] Even if we can't *stop* child abuse, we can do our part to *prevent* it, and we can reach out with loving hands to *put back together the lives* of the children who have suffered abuse. That's why we wanted to write this book.

In the following chapters you'll learn about the devastating long-term effects that child abuse has on its victims. You'll see the inspirational model God has established for us to follow in responding to this crisis. You'll learn practical steps that the church can take both to mend the broken lives of abused children and to help abusers overcome their terrible struggle. Finally, you'll be introduced to Royal Family Kids' Camps, one avenue of healing we as Christians have created for abused children.

Throughout this book you'll meet the children behind the shocking statistics, children like the two young girls Johanna met one day at the Orange County, California, courthouse.

Johanna and her husband, Jim, are actively involved with children's ministry both at their church and with our camps for abused kids. It seemed natural for them to take the next step and become foster parents. To prepare for this responsibility, Johanna and Jim attended classes at the Orange County courthouse.

One day as Johanna walked past one of the courtrooms, she heard voices calling to her: "Johanna! Do you remember us? We know you! Do you remember?"

Turning to see two young girls calling her, Johanna couldn't place their faces. When she hesitated, they shouted, "We were at camp with you. Remember?" The young girls were in court for another legal gambit in their foster situation. Johanna began to chat with them as they waited for the elevator. "We remember all the songs you taught us at camp," they bubbled. "Come on, sing them with us!" they prodded.

It had been six months since camp. Johanna didn't think they could remember too many of the songs. Right in the courthouse hall, she joined them in singing the camp theme song; then they broke into

My Father's rich in houses and land;
He holds the wealth of the world in His hands! . . .
I'm a child of the King wherever I go.

They remembered every word of seven songs. That's how important camp had been to them.

Children like these two young girls have little in this world. They don't ask us for very much. They deeply appreciate and love anything we can give them. The following pages will introduce you to more of these special children and show you how to help them.

CHAPTER TWO

A Lifetime of Scars: The Long-Term Effects of Child Abuse

FRANKY was seven years old when his Sunday school class went Christmas caroling at a rest home in town. No different from any other inquisitive young boy, Franky wandered away from the group and went exploring. Those were his last moments as a bright, outgoing child. An elderly male resident grabbed Franky and dragged him into his shower stall, where he beat him, sodomized him, and performed various other horrifying acts on Franky's little body. Forty-five minutes later, Franky's Sunday school teacher found him wandering outside the rest home. He was bloodied, bruised, and so traumatized that he couldn't even cry.

By the time Franky turned eight, he had attempted suicide three times. The impact of child abuse is tragic. Sometimes the scars can last a lifetime.

We first learned about Franky while he was hospitalized in a psychiatric ward because of his suicidal tendencies. His doctors thought a change of scenery might help, and they wanted to send him to a summer camp for abused children. If you had met Franky that summer, his terrible fears and insecurities would have reduced you to tears. That young boy—at eight years old—was afraid to use the bathroom because he had been abused in a bathroom. He made his camp counselor stand guard every time he had to go to the bathroom. He refused to take a shower throughout the entire week he was at camp.

The victims of child abuse in general and sexual abuse in particular have so many ongoing problems to deal with, and poor Franky needs help every step of the way. His church has provided wonderful counseling for him, and he continued to return every summer to Royal Family Kids' Camps. The third year we were delighted to see Franky running to greet us the first morning of camp. His cheerful face told us that he had big news for us. He said, "You know that man who did all those things to me? Well, I've forgiven him."

What a lesson Franky taught us that day. What would it have taken to make us forgive someone who had hurt us the way Franky had been hurt? What would it have taken to make you forgive? But Franky was learning to forgive, and the healing in his life had begun.

When Franky was twelve, the last year he was eligible for camp, he had begun to grow up and look forward to a career that would make him a rich person. As it turned out, his camp counselor that year, Dan, was an investment counselor. This fascinated Franky, who had become devoted to his goal of future wealth. Dan finally asked him, "Franky, what do you want all that money for?"

Franky grinned. "I want to *buy* Royal Family Kids' Camps," he said.

"Why would you want to buy the camp?" Dan asked.

"So I can make sure other kids can have the same safe feelings I've had when I've come here," Franky said. Franky is as close to a success story as we come in this business. He still has a lot of problems to work through.

In addition to the scars left by physical pain and anguish, child abuse also leaves emotional scars.

Scar #1: Death of Trust

Because so often child abuse and neglect involve the child's caregiver, trust is one of the major casualties in the battle. The first person children trust in their lives is the hand that rocks the cradle. What then becomes of trust if that hand also breaks, bruises, and maims?

Young children come to recognize that the one person on whom they should be able to rely for love and protection is actually the enemy. They cannot rely on their caregivers to protect them, so they must learn to protect themselves. This mistrust of the primary adults in their lives is often transferred to all adults. If their parents, grandparents, and stepparents aren't to be trusted, then no one is.

This distrust is demonstrated at lights-out time at our camp. At *any* kids' camp, lights-out time is rowdy enough, with no dorm full of children wanting to settle down and end a day of fun one moment before they absolutely have to. But at a camp for abused children, this problem is even more intensified. For many of our young campers, abuse at home begins when the lights go out. Sexual abuse in particular may be strongly associated with the dark and silence. The children are reluctant to sleep because they fear an abuser might try to hurt them. Dreams and nightmares also haunt many of the children.

For these reasons, we start our lights-out procedures early in the evening to give the campers lots of time to settle in and get to sleep. The very first year of camp, as I (Wayne) made rounds to help the counselors get the boys to bed, I noticed that Alan was sleeping with his head on the Bible he had received earlier in the day. When I saw Alan the next morning, I asked him why he was using his Bible as a pillow. "Oh," he said, "it makes me feel safe to sleep with my head on the Bible."

For Alan, sleeping on the Scriptures made him feel safe, but many abused children never feel safe again, by day or by night. Some young children sleep with layers of clothes on to make molestation more difficult. For some children, even the casual touch of an adult is a cause for hysteria. Many of the children have an impaired capacity for intimacy. Their innocence and childhood have been murdered.

Scar #2: Perpetual Anger

Children in our society are taught to honor adults. Because of the size difference between children and adults, children realize that they can't defend themselves against an adult attacker. It is impossible for children to vindicate themselves on an adult who is abusing them. The result is a perpetual anger that has no avenue for expression. As adults, we know that pent-up anger must be released, or it will work itself out in ways that are generally not related to the subject of the anger. Abused children handle their anger in the same way.

Whereas an adult stands a fighting chance of escaping abuse or overcoming abusers, children have no such hope. The situation of an abused child is analogous to that of a mouse in a trap: The mouse is in constant pain, but it cannot escape. Terrifying rage can result.

Children who have been abused *ought* to be angry about it. This anger, which cannot be directed toward the adult abuser, is then funneled wherever it can go. Peer relationships can be devastated, for abused children cannot relate to other children without their powerful anger interfering. Many abused children act out at school and on the playground, letting their misplaced aggressions destroy their friendships.

If the abuse is not addressed, the anger becomes bitterness. As Christians, we are well aware of the damage that bitterness can do in our souls. The Bible tells us not even to let one day pass with bitterness in our hearts. For abused children, bitterness becomes a way of life. It is not really shocking that the only way out of the bitterness and anger for some children is suicide. For others, this rage can turn outward: Many convicted serial killers have been the victims of child abuse.

Because abused children are forced to swallow their true feelings, especially feelings of anger, they are often incapable of identifying their true feelings themselves.[1]

At the RFKC camp in Poulsbo, Washington, an eight-year-old girl demonstrated this kind of anger by "shredding" a bench built of two-by-fours. After an RFKC staff member reported the damage to the camp manager and offered to pay for the damage, the camp manager said it was not necessary to replace the bench. The manager's only concern was how the young girl was doing.

Scar #3: Self-Hatred

The developmental years of children's lives determine their self-image. Young children tend to regard any pain or unpleasantness in their lives as their own fault. Many, many abused children believe the abuse happens because they are in some way bad or have done something bad—particularly because much abuse happens in the name of punishment for misdeeds.

I'm reminded of Mindy, who came to camp. "I'm no good at anything," she said. "My mommy says I'm no good. I can't swim or do anything right."

As Mindy's camp counselor heard these words, she thought, *It breaks my heart to hear Mindy say those things. What kind of world would cause so much hurt inside someone so young?*

Thankfully, Mindy's life was put back on track through her experience at camp. The second night of her stay, she told her counselor, "I want Jesus to be my friend." But that wasn't the only change in Mindy's life that week. She also learned to swim.

"I am so good!" she declared to her counselor on Thursday. "I can swim so good. I'm good at everything!" Too many abused children never make the discovery that Mindy made. For them, their self-image has died painfully.

If abused children believe that abuse is their fault because they are bad, they often abandon themselves to this "badness" and let it become a self-fulfilling prophecy. Abused children express their self-hatred through self-destructive behavior. Some of them subconsciously set themselves up for abuse, thinking they somehow deserve it because they are "bad."

Abused children internalize their feelings of helplessness

and isolation only to find that these feelings haunt them throughout their lives. Because many abused children are forced to go to great lengths to try to hide what is happening to them, they may be forced to withdraw from normal peer relationships at an early age. They may find themselves isolated and cut off from those they see as normal.

This isolation can result in many sad, lost years, and it may manifest itself differently in boys and girls, mainly because of the prevailing attitudes about male and female roles in our society. Even today in America, girls are raised to be more caring and gentle, "weaker" if you will, than boys. Young girls who are abused may turn into "permanent victims." Boys in our society, on the other hand, are socialized to be more aggressive and physical than girls are. A boy who has been abused may respond with hostility and aggression.[2] Furthermore, the abused boy may become the one who victimizes others. This is evident in the high number of male convicts who were abused as children: Two of every three prisoners convicted of first-degree murder report childhood histories of physical abuse.[3]

Although the scars of child abuse are varied and complex, they can be healed. The church can and ought to be part of the healing process. The church can become the arms of the Lord taking care of neglected children as the psalmist expresses: "When my father and my mother forsake me, then the Lord will take care of me" (Ps. 27:10, NKJV).

Through his body, the church, the Lord has taken care of people like Lisa. Lisa was removed from her abusive home when she was young, and she never lived with her own family again. We met her when she attended the first camp that we ever sponsored for abused kids. She was small, frightened, and embarrassed that the other kids would notice and make fun of her hearing aids.

At that point in her young life, Lisa could have taken many paths, some of which would have left deep scars. But through God's grace, Lisa found help and healing long before her scars became permanent. At camp she met one of the camp grandpas and was thrilled to see that he wore hearing aids too. She also learned of the love of Jesus and accepted him as her Savior. That was six years ago. Lisa, now seventeen, has goals and is working to make a future for herself.

Like Franky, Lisa is working toward becoming a success story among abused children. She's going to make it. She's going to be a strong, healthy, Christian young woman. For others, the story won't be nearly as cheerful. And although we perhaps cannot make the difference for all the millions of children who will be abused this year, the church, working together, can make the difference for *some* of them.

CHAPTER THREE

Royal Family Kids' Camps: One Small Way to Make a Big Difference

IF the decision had been ours to make, we would have filled this book with photographs of the battered and abused children we know—not photographs of their bruises or their blood or their crying faces twisted in pain, but of their happy smiles at summer camp, their faces lit up with joy as they make crafts or play games, their eyes lifted toward heaven as they sing songs and worship God. Those photographs, more than almost anything we could say to you, would have convinced you that these kids deserve our help. There's nothing like seeing a genuine grin on the face of a girl or boy who had almost forgotten how to smile.

Unfortunately we can't fill this book with pictures of those children because most of them are in the foster-care system of the state where they live. We had to change their names in this book to tell their stories, and to preserve their confidentiality even further, we can't let you see the pictures of their precious faces. But we can describe for you this fact: For many of them, the happiest week of their entire year is the week they spend at Royal Family Kids' Camps. We want to tell you about RFKC because it is a small example of how some people who care about abused kids have made an incredible impact in their lives. These people are not psychologists, doctors, or public lobbyists but ordinary people like you.

Royal Family Kids' Camps

The very first RFKC camp was sponsored in 1985 by Newport-Mesa Christian Center in Costa Mesa, California. I (Wayne) was on staff with the church, and as I see now, God had planted in my heart a dream to reach out to help children whose lives had been devastated by abuse and neglect. I can still remember a vision God gave me when I was only twelve years old. The vision showed a sea of faces of children from all nationalities and races. That vision became reality during the first RFKC.

During that first week of camp, the needs of the children touched the hearts of all of us who worked at camp. We realized that if other churches got behind a program like RFKC, we could reach hundreds of abused children every year. So we began to challenge other churches to follow this simple model: Organize a one-week summer camp for abused children in your area. Child-protective agencies and foster families are eager to send children because abused and neglected children miss many normal childhood experiences.

To demonstrate the family concept for children whose families have been horribly broken, we try to create a family atmosphere. Each RFKC camp includes on the staff a grandma and grandpa and an aunt and uncle. Their roles are simply to love the children, affirm them, tell them stories, and, of course, to have a heart big enough to be broken many times before the week is over. Children warm up quickly to gray hair and a sincere hug. Before long, they are pouring out their hearts to Grandma and Grandpa. For many of our children, these are the only grandparents they will ever know or be in contact with.

In addition to the normal recreational activities of summer camp, each week of RFKC is designed around a biblical teaching that challenges the abused or neglected child to draw close to God. For instance, one standard curriculum for camp focuses on Joseph. Can you think of any biblical hero to whom abused kids might relate better? Joseph was injured by his own family, cast into a deep pit, and sold into slavery. A foster child knows and understands how Joseph felt when he was abused, removed from his home, and forced to live in a foreign land.

We design our camps to help abused children recover by addressing the very issues that are most important for them. For instance, one of the worst results of child abuse is children's loss of self-esteem and their feeling that something must be wrong with them to have brought this abuse on themselves. The Cambridge Graduate School of Psychology recommends that abused children be given activities that they can successfully complete. At RFKC the crafts and sports are all designed to help children do well and feel good about their performance. Counselors and other staff members reinforce good effort, teaching children that they are good and worthy of love and affection.

We want the children to understand that they're not worthless, that in God's sight they are precious. Abused children feel like losers before they have even begun to play the game. It's important for us to help them realize that they are winners! Even the name of our camp—Royal Family—is designed to make our campers feel special. We believe that Jesus sees them as royalty because they are joint heirs with him.

Abused children also suffer a loss of trust and the anxiety of never feeling safe. At RFKC they meet caring Christian adults who can be trusted and with whom they are safe. One year Laurie came to camp wearing about six layers of clothing; she refused to take off any of her clothes because dressing in several layers had been her only defense against her father's sexual advances and inappropriate touching. Laurie had a boy's haircut, and she did her best to appear to be a rough-and-tumble tomboy in an effort to discourage men from taking an interest in her.

Laurie's camp counselor assured her that she didn't need to wear all those clothes all the time, but Laurie wouldn't even change clothes with anyone near her. She continued to dress in layers until halfway into camp, when she finally realized that no one was going to hurt her. One night she decided she would put on her pajamas for bed. As she appeared in the dorm in a silky pink nightgown, she said to her counselor, "See, I really *am* a pretty girl."

It speaks volumes that a child like Laurie felt safe enough to let down her guard with her counselor and friends at RFKC. In ways like this the camp staff tries to rebuild the trust of children who have been abused.

Another problem that many abused children may suffer is an inability to interact with peers. Constant attempts to hide abuse can make them unable to relate to their peers in a normal way. Plus, they often cope with a conscious feeling that they aren't normal, which can make them afraid to reach out to children they perceive as normal. Royal Family Kids' Camps addresses that problem by helping children develop caring relationships with each other.

Jill, who holds a master's degree in social work and who is a caseworker for a nonprofit agency in her state, has worked as a camp counselor. She wrote to me: "One thing I have noticed about older foster children is that they usually have seen or know each other. When they see another child familiar to them, they usually say, 'Were you at Orangewood?' or 'I think I know you.' But now for some of the older foster children, that question is changing to 'Weren't you at Royal Family Kids' Camps last summer?' These children are making their own special clique from their camping experience. It's wonderful to see how RFKC is making an impact on the children's friendships and relationships with others, even outside of the camp."

One Week Makes a Difference

We have no doubt at all that one week at Royal Family Kids' Camps can change the life of an abused child forever, if for no other reason than the fact that they are introduced to Christ Jesus, whose healing love is the most important ingredient in successful living.

Take Skip, a twelve-year-old boy who was attending his final year of camp. (To be eligible for RFKC, a child must be between ages seven and twelve.) Every year the camp staff hosts a party called "Everybody's Birthday Party" because many children in foster care and group homes never have a birthday celebration. The party includes cake, candles, party decorations, presents—the works! It was the night of Everybody's Birthday Party, but Skip wasn't enjoying himself. Glenn, the camp director, saw that Skip was upset, and he asked him what was wrong.

Skip told him he was sad because it was the last night of his last week at camp, probably forever. But then he turned to Glenn and said with the real conviction of a twelve-year-old, "Glenn, if you ever visit my neighborhood and see me walking down the street, you'll see a man of God walking toward you."

That's the most important mission of Royal Family Kids' Camps: to let the kids know that they are God's children.

In chapter 1 you met Carey, whose abusive father had committed suicide after murdering Carey's nine-year-old brother and trying to kill his seven-year-old brother and Carey. Five years after his father had tried to kill him, Carey had become morose, withdrawn, and sad. Terrible nightmares haunted his sleep, and he couldn't conquer a bed-wetting problem. After his first week at RFKC, Carey's mother noticed a remarkable change in her son. He came bounding into her room, wanting to return to camp again the following week. When she asked him why he enjoyed camp so much, he said, "Because up there *everybody* loves me!"

Three months later Carey's mother told me, "You'll never know what your camp has meant to our family. Carey is like a new child! He used to be sullen and withdrawn. These days I've heard him bouncing through the house, *singing* the songs you taught him at camp."

Side Effects

Another positive result of Royal Family Kids' Camps is that some counselors choose to become foster parents.

Already five couples who acted as counselors at one camp have attained foster-care status. These couples are also exposing the people in their churches to the needy kids in the system, hoping to inspire other couples to become foster parents. There is an urgent need for foster parents, and caring Christian families are some of the best possible places for foster children to learn of God's love for them.

One family that felt this impact was the Carlsons. Rick Carlson had been a camp counselor, and he continued to maintain contact with Jerry, one of the boys he had been in charge of during his week at RFKC. Rick says, "I was beginning to like this little guy, and I really wished I could be his dad. My wife, Joan, and I often had discussed the subject of a son during our fifteen years of marriage. We already had two beautiful daughters."

Rick and Joan decided to look into the possibility of adopting Jerry. Of course, that's not exactly how the adoption process works. Generally potential adoptive parents are not allowed to preselect a child, especially in the state foster-care system. But the Carlsons took the chance. Jerry's social worker told them they could submit an application to adopt, but it was almost certain to be a fruitless effort. The system is designed to find the best placement for the child, she said. If potential adoptive parents know the child beforehand, that relationship can severely limit the system's ability to place the child in the best circumstances.

In the months following their application, the Carlsons learned that the foster family with whom Jerry had been staying planned to adopt him. The Carlsons had never mentioned to Jerry that they were investigating the possibility of adopting him. They were happy that he would finally become a real member of his foster family. "I felt good about Jerry's future," Rick says. "At the same time, I felt a deep sadness because I knew I would miss him."

More than a year after Jerry's camp experience and seven months after the Carlsons had applied to become adoptive parents, Jerry's foster mother called Rick to say that they were giving Jerry up. She wanted the Carlsons to take him. The social-service agency again discouraged this.

"They were frank with us," Rick says. "They told us all of Jerry's problems and described all the possible drawbacks. The picture they painted seemed to be a bleak one. They had almost no hope for this child. They said Jerry had been diagnosed with attention deficit hyperactivity disorder (ADHD), and his IQ had been tested and was in the borderline retarded range. They told us they felt it was next to impossible for Jerry to bond with anyone, that all of his time in foster care had robbed him of his ability to fit into a normal family. Their recommendation was to place him in a group home with full-time psychiatric staffing.

"But I thought they were misreading Jerry," Rick Carlson recounts. "In all the time we had spent together—our time in camp and my follow-up interaction with him—I had a sense of Jerry's spirit, and I knew he had one tremendous asset. He had a good heart."

Joan and Rick Carlson adopted Jerry early in 1989. During the next few months the Carlsons and Jerry worked on Jerry's ADHD with a special California State University program, where they discovered that many of Jerry's problems stemmed from an undiagnosed case of Tourette's syndrome, a neurological disorder that can cause involuntary muscle and vocal action. The disorder was made worse by drug therapy Jerry had received for his hyperactivity.

With this new information and therapy to help deal with his problems, Jerry began to learn and grow rapidly, and he gradually became a genuine part of the family. That year on Father's Day, Jerry asked Joan to help him shop for a special gift for Rick. He wanted to get him a picture frame like one he had seen his foster sister give her father. "When we were all together, all the kids gave me their gifts," Rick said. "Jerry held his for last. When I opened it, I discovered a framed picture of Jerry and me at camp when he was my camper."

"I never had a dad before, and now you're my dad," Jerry told Rick as they shared a big hug.

Jerry attends junior high now. He has been honored as the citizen of the month there and recently made the principal's list for his 3.0 grade-point average. "We were proud of him," Rick says. "We marveled at the change in Jerry, who not long ago was considered to have a low IQ and was seen as uneducable. He has since tested in the high IQ range and is considered to be very bright. But I had known that about Jerry ever since I met him at camp."

For Jerry, the camp experience had a life-changing impact. Not all children will find such dramatic results from camp, but for hundreds of them each summer, camp does make a real difference.

Not everyone will feel called to become foster parents as the Carlsons have, but you can do *something* to help abused children. You don't have to be an expert. You just have to be a compassionate Christian who cares for children.

"A wide door for effective work has opened to me, and there are many adversaries," Paul wrote in 1 Corinthians 16:9

(NRSV). The door is wide open for bringing abused children to Christ. Thousands of them are in group homes and foster homes throughout our land, and they need the Lord's loving touch. There are indeed many adversaries, for I believe that Satan enjoys abused children's pain and thrives on their broken hearts. But we can overcome the adversaries, and we can change life forever for these children.

When the four stretcher-bearers in the account recorded in the Gospel of Mark arrived at the house in which Jesus was teaching, they faced many adversaries; they couldn't even get through the door. But they didn't allow that to stop them because they wanted to get their sick friend to Jesus. The four men dug through a roof to do it. Let's be willing to work as hard for the broken and battered children who need our help.

Becoming a Royal Family Kids' Camps volunteer opens the door of awareness to child-abuse issues. But many counselors and staff members want to do more throughout the year.

In Poulsbo, Washington, volunteers from Christ Memorial Church became interested in setting up an Adopt-a-Social-Worker program in their community, providing year-round response to very practical needs that a social worker might encounter—supplying a bed, a dresser, a bicycle, needed clothing, etc.

In Phoenix, Arizona, the nine-church coalition that sponsors an RFKC camp became active year-round when fifty volunteers received training in crisis intervention to help at-risk families.

In Puyallup, Washington, the camp director, Merrilee, became the "shopper" for the director of the child-protective services, shopping for clothing items that would be distributed to needy children within the director's jurisdiction—a much needed helping hand in this overloaded position within the child-protective services agency.

Royal Family Kids' Camps is a thriving example of how the church can make a difference in the lives of children who have been battered and abused. If you and your church are interested in learning more about RFKC or even sponsoring a camp in your area, please call or write us at Royal Family Kids' Camps, Inc., 1068 Salinas Avenue, Costa Mesa, California 92626, (714) 556-1420.

CHAPTER FOUR

An Unsung Heroes Hall of Fame

WHEN I was a boy growing up in upstate New York, the Baseball Hall of Fame in Cooperstown held special memories for me. I was a young baseball-card collector, and walking the halls of the Baseball Hall of Fame helped me envision awe-inspiring actions on the ball diamond. As an adult, I visited the Basketball Hall of Fame in Springfield, Massachusetts. I shot hoops in a special interactive display and saw the beat-up peach basket that Dr. James Naismith used when he invented the game.

Let me introduce you to another hall of fame.

In 1990 Diane and I sat in the morning service in a Southern California church that had just sponsored its first RFKC camp. The speaker asked all the adults involved in the camp to come forward. As those forty people stood in the front, the speaker declared, "The people that stand before you today are the unsung heroes of the faith. They are the ones who had the courage and the heart to step into the unknown and come back victors." At that proclamation, the congregation of two thousand people stood to their feet and applauded these volunteers. As we sat in the back of the church, we looked at the people who surrounded us and saw tears rolling down their faces. God's power was nearly tangible in that moment. Those forty people could easily be anonymous in a church the size of that one. For that one moment, everyone saw their faces and recognized their extraordinary commitment. These are some of the unsung heroes in the Royal Family Kids' Camps Hall of Fame.

The Bible has a hall of fame too. While Hebrews 11 names specific men and women who stepped out in faith—Abraham, Jacob, Joseph, Moses, Gideon, Sarah, Samson, and David—the Bible also includes many unsung heroes whose great deeds we remember even though we don't know their names.

In 1 Samuel 14 we read the story of Saul's son Jonathan and a young man with no other name than "the young man bearing his armor." These two young men attacked a Philistine garrison by themselves, "The Philistines fell before Jonathan, and his armor-bearer followed and killed behind him. . . . Then panic struck the whole army . . . and the ground shook. It was a panic sent by God" (1 Sam. 14:13-15). Jonathan and this nameless armor-bearer were so successful that the entire Philistine army finally ran away. But we don't know the armor-bearer's name.

A key player in the story of Christ's feeding the five thousand is a nameless young boy. Faced with the needs of a hungry crowd, Jesus told his disciples to feed them. "Andrew, Simon Peter's brother, spoke up, 'Here is a boy with five small barley loaves and two small fish, but how far will they go among so many?'" (John 6:8-9). Then Jesus took the boy's lunch and multiplied it to feed the hungry people. And when all the people were satisfied, the disciples collected twelve basketfuls of leftover food. All that bread and fish started out as one boy's lunch. He was as hungry as anyone else, but he gave his meal to Jesus. Although this miracle is recorded in every Gospel, the boy is mentioned in only John's record, and his name is never given.

The Samaritan woman who spoke with Jesus at the well is another unnamed person of faith. When Jesus explained to her that he could give her living water—himself—she believed him and went to get her friends and neighbors. As the result of her belief, "Many of the Samaritans from that town believed in him" (John 4:39). She was an effective evangelist, yet no one recorded her name.

We don't know the name of the widow who gave generously out of her poverty. But Jesus said of her, "This poor widow has put more into the treasury than all the others. They all gave out of their wealth; but she, out of her poverty, put in everything—all she had to live on" (Mark 12:43-44). We all remember her story, but no one knows her name.

In Ecclesiastes 9:14-15, we read, "There was once a small city with only a few people in it. And a powerful king came against it, surrounded it and built huge siegeworks against it. Now there lived in that city a man poor but wise, and he saved the city by his wisdom. But nobody remembered that poor man." No one remembered his name.

We consider this man the model for all the unsung heroes in our Royal Family Kids' Camps Hall of Fame. His situation closely mirrors ours. His city contained few soldiers, but it was surrounded by a powerful army. As this book has demonstrated, the problems of child abuse and neglect are overwhelming our nation. People are besieged with child abuse and its lifelong aftereffects on survivors, just as the city in Ecclesiastes was besieged by a powerful king.

Inside the city walls of that biblical city, people were looking for anyone who had great wisdom. They gave up asking their own king and the wise men of his royal court; they didn't have the answers. They turned instead to a poor man, a man who had no reputation, who had no great name or flamboyant career as a wise man. Yet he was the one who delivered the city, the Scripture tells us. A poor but wise man.

People who volunteer at Royal Family Kids' Camps and the family of contributors who finance the camps are following the lead of this poor wise man. Most of them are not experts in psychology or child abuse, but they make a wise choice. They choose to follow the command of Christ, who asked us to bring the little children to him.

We count the RFKC camp directors, staff, counselors, grandmas and grandpas, and donors as unsung heroes. Their names may one day be forgotten, but their heroic deeds will live on in the hearts and minds of children. We want to tell some of their stories, to list here a small fraction of the names that should be inscribed in the Unsung Heroes Hall of Fame.

Members of the RFKC Hall of Fame

GLENN GARVIN knows how the children of Royal Family Kids' Camps feel because he has been there. His parents separated when he was a baby, and for a time he was raised by his father, a heroin and cocaine addict. When Glenn was four years old, he was adopted by a different family, but the father of this family was abusive. The marriage broke up, and Glenn's adoptive father committed suicide when Glenn was twelve years old.

"The difference between Royal Family kids and me is that they have been pulled out of the home for their own protection, and I wasn't. But I can relate to their fear and insecurity. My past has given me a lot of understanding for these kids," Glenn says. "It helps me work more effectively with them."

Glenn, a camp director from Lakewood, California, has been involved with the program for six years. Glenn is one of our unsung heroes. He tells the story of Skip, a ten-year-old camper who wore gang clothing and symbols. "That year several of the kids seemed to be in a gang mode," Glenn says. "One day a camper named Carl said something about Skip's mother, and the two boys were ready to come to blows. It was as if Skip actually wanted to kill Carl for talking about his mother."

Glenn sat down with Skip and tried to calm him down. "I told him not to take it so personally. Carl didn't even know his mother, so how could he say what she was like? Skip told me that just one week earlier, he had watched his father shoot his mother. She died. Then he watched the police take his father away. Skip said he planned to kill his dad when he got out of prison."

The stories and struggles of the campers at Royal Family Kids' Camps are very different from the stories counselors can expect to hear at a normal summer camp. Glenn and the staff continued to work with Skip, and by the end of the week, Skip cried because he had to leave his counselor. He seemed ready to love again.

"One year later, Skip returned to camp," Glenn says. "He

got on the bus at church a different boy! He was eleven years old now, and he talked to the younger boys, telling them how great camp was and how they were going to love it. It turned out that instead of being the problem he had been the year before, he was like a big brother to the other kids. He helped with cleanup, worked with other kids, and took a lot of responsibility."

Glenn Garvin and the staff of the Lakewood camp, you are heroes to that young man. You are unsung heroes.

LINDA CHEELEY is director of the RFKC camp in Phoenix, Arizona. This camp has developed the family concept of Royal Family even more by calling their camp counselors "camp cousins." The children feel right at home from the start, except for one incorrigible child we'll call Max. The first thing Max did at camp was to organize a group of malcontents and try to run away. When Max and his friends were discovered and convinced to remain at camp, Max said, "This place is a living hell."

The camp's dean of men told him, "If you think this place is hell, you must have a pretty wonderful life."

Max shook his head. "Not quite," he said. Max continued to be a problem. Throughout the week Linda helped the camp staff deal with Max's anger, poor behavior, and bad language. When the awards for camp cousins were being presented, Max asked Linda if she would receive one. She told him the awards were only for cousins, not for the camp director. Max objected, "Well, you *should* get an award. You've done a really good job."

In her years of directing RFKC camps, Linda has heard and seen a lot of moving moments. She was surprised when a case manager asked if one camper could return to camp—a year after she had reached our upper age limit of twelve. "The child was being pulled between her birth mother and a foster home, and her case manager thought another year of camp would be good for her," Linda says. "The girl had a learning disability, and they told me she had been reading her Bible all year since she received it at the last year's camp."

One time during Everybody's Birthday Party, a young girl told Linda how excited she had been on her tenth birthday because she was finally two digits old. But her real birthday had been lonely because her mother had been in jail and her mother's male friend merely had flipped a nickel to her and told her to have a happy birthday. No party, no gifts, no cake. But she received all of those things at the camp birthday party. "After the party, she said she felt as if she finally was ten years old," Linda reports.

Linda says the camp cousins and staff of the Phoenix, Arizona, camp give their hearts. "And sometimes their hearts break," she adds. Thank you, Linda and Phoenix staff, for allowing your hearts to be broken on behalf of children who need you. You are heroes!

LYNELL BROOKS, a personal friend, has been the camp nurse of the original camp sponsored by Newport-Mesa Christian Center. Lynell jokes that she went to lunch with us one day and ended up drafted to serve at the camp! Before coming to RFKC, Lynell had worked with us in other camps. She comments on the differences she sees between RFKC and other camps: "We thought we knew what we were doing. One counselor for every two campers sounded easy! But working at RFKC was the hardest thing I have ever done in my life. I wasn't prepared for the emotional wringer. These children were nothing like the kids at other camps at which I had worked. Along the way somewhere, some adult has changed the course of history for them."

Lynell observes about RFKC campers, "As a camp nurse, I have found these kids don't need much nursing. They aren't used to being 'mothered' every time they have an ache or pain. Other kids come to the camp nurse for every little thing, but RFKC kids just tough it out and think they should take care of themselves. Nurturing is so foreign to them."

The same principle applies to the food, Lynell reports. Usually, kids at regular camps complain about the food constantly. "RFKC campers eat it and love it. Many campers hoard the food, stuffing their pockets with food from the table since they often don't know where their next meal is coming from. They have to be reminded that another meal will be served in a few hours."

The first day of camp, when the buses arrive, is Lynell's favorite part of camp. The kids, counselors, and staff are filled with emotion. "When I see them piling off the bus, I can notice how much they have grown. It's heartwarming to watch the kids run to find their counselors. It's as if they're coming home. For many of the children, we are the only consistent thing in their lives, sometimes the only thing they can really count on."

Like almost everyone involved in Royal Family, Lynell says life is never quite the same after a week of camp. "It opens my eyes to realities I never would have known about. These kids are in our schools and our foster-care systems, and we never know their pain. I feel angry to think how adults can do such horrible things to innocent children. Through working at Royal Family Kids' Camps, I have grown more compassionate and aware."

When Lynell's daughter was seven years old, a seven-year-old camper came to the nurse's office at camp. The girl had been taken from her family and placed in a county shelter because of her parents' drug use. She was new to the foster-care system, a little sick, and very scared. The parallels between Lynell's seven-year-old daughter and this seven-year-old girl struck her. "I just wanted to take this child home, but I couldn't," she says. "We learn to trust in the sovereignty of God as we try to love and care for these children because we don't always have the answers."

Lynell, you and the staff of the Newport-Mesa camp may not have all the answers, but you are heroes!

MERRILEE MORRELL says the real heroes of Royal Family Kids' Camps are the counselors. "They are with the kids almost twenty-four hours a day. The kids confide in them, so they carry a heavy load," Merrilee says. "On the last day of camp, it's very hard to say good-bye. Every counselor cries, and no one is really prepared to let go."

I met Merrilee, who is the director of our first camp in Puyallup, Washington, at a conference for children's pastors. We were impressed with her dedication to helping abused children. After meeting us and hearing about Royal Family Kids' Camps, Merrilee and her husband, a children's pastor at Puyallup Church of the Nazarene, made the commitment to reach out to the abused and neglected kids of their area. That commitment has grown and blossomed.

"Royal Family Kids' Camps has made me even more of an advocate for the children," Merrilee says. "We had foster children in our Christmas program at church this year, and the social-service agencies were so thrilled with the camp that they asked us to develop a Christmas program for other kids in the system. In our county alone, seventeen hundred children are under state care. The social-service workers tell us that five hundred of these kids will never have a birthday party or a present. We want to help these kids not only at camp but also during the rest of the year."

Merrilee says her favorite part of camp is seeing the changes in the children. Since RFKC was new to the children of Puyallup last summer, the children arrived very wary and distrustful. "When they got off the bus, they seemed to have one of two expressions on their faces: anger or a kind of hollow look," Merrilee says. "But by the end of the week, their faces were shining. They had happy, smiling eyes. One young boy tried to hide so he wouldn't have to go home."

The agent who rented the campground to RFKC said he was amazed that five days had made such a difference in the way children acted and responded.

"One nine-year-old boy started right out letting everybody know that he couldn't care less about being at camp," Merrilee reports. "But by the end of the week, his apathy had changed to interest. He kept asking if he could come back next year."

Similar transformations happened throughout the camp. A seven-year-old girl who had been sexually abused would not let anyone touch her. Yet by the end of the camp, she was running to the camp grandma and grandpa to give them hugs.

Two little guys at lunch held up their drinking glasses, clinked them together in a toast, and declared, "To the best days of our lives!"

An eight-year-old girl reported to her social worker, "You know, I'm special. I didn't think so, but they told me so at camp, and I believe it." Merrilee and Puyallup staff, to that young girl who hadn't even known that she is special, you are heroes!

SANDI HAMLIN did something you've probably done with your children and grandchildren. Sandi took a young girl with an injured ankle to the emergency room. Because she had read the girl's camp application and file, Sandi knew that when this young girl was only three years old, her mother had abandoned her. Sandi understood why the girl screamed almost nonstop when she was placed on the gurney to be taken for treatment. She wouldn't calm down until Sandi had taken her hand and had stayed with her the entire time. Afterward, Sandi said, "You were afraid I would leave you, weren't you?"

The young girl answered, "Yes. My mother did. Thank you for not leaving me."

Sandi didn't start out with much dedication to Royal Family Kids' Camps. When her pastor first asked her to be involved, she agreed with reservations. "I guess I wasn't convinced that anything could be accomplished with these kids in five days," she says. "But after the training camp and observation, I came home absolutely convinced. I plan to be a part of Royal Family Kids' Camps as long as I can because it's so important for these children to learn about Jesus. When I see the expression in their eyes, it makes it really worth it."

Sandi says her favorite part of camp is Everybody's Birthday Party. The hall is decorated, and a huge cake shines with one candle for every child present. "We let the youngest child blow the candles out," Sandi says. "Most of these children have never had a party before. Because we don't tell the children about the party ahead of time, it's a surprise when they walk into the hall. They are just shocked to think it's a celebration for everybody's birthday."

Sandi's husband and daughter are also involved with Royal Family Kids' Camps today. "Having worked with RFKC has changed my perception of my own church. We're a small congregation of about 250, but we have really rallied around abused children. We have done a lot with very little."

For doing so much for the children, Sandi and her church congregation deserve a place in our Unsung Heroes Hall of Fame.

Sandi's small church, which is making such a *big difference* in the lives of abused children, is First Christian Church in St. Joseph, Missouri. I (Wayne) was traveling Interstate 29 north from Kansas City to St. Joseph one time when an unusual sight caught my eyes. Three red-tailed hawks were sitting on fenceposts, not in the trees or on the tops of telephone poles, where these hawks usually perch. When I described the scene to the pastor of First Christian Church, he said the hawks have become "buzzardized." Instead of flying at high altitudes, like the great aerial hunters they were designed to be, the hawks of that region are content with perching on fenceposts close to the highway. He went on to explain that fenceposts provide easy access to "roadkill"—animals that have been run over by cars. He calls it "buzzard mentality," waiting for someone else to do the work.

Some Christians, although created and designed by God to reach great heights and accomplish great deeds, are satisfied just to sit in a pew and wait for others to do the ministry. They have allowed themselves to become buzzardized.

Not so with the people involved in Royal Family Kids' Camps. Rather than sitting on the fenceposts waiting to hear about God's wonderful healing for abused children, they are actively involved in making a difference in children's lives. They give their prayers, time, talent, and resources; they encourage new staff members or get their own churches involved. Through it all, they are soaring to new heights. They explore and examine the many possibilities for new ministries, and they seize opportunities to participate in great and small ways.

Don't sit on the fencepost, waiting for your roadkill. Join the Unsung Heroes Hall of Fame. Make a difference by following the dream and playing the role that God has appointed for you!

CHAPTER FIVE

Memories for a Lifetime

ONE evening in July 1993, I (Diane) replayed the video of our September 16, 1990, farewell celebration service from Newport-Mesa Christian Center, where Wayne had served as senior associate pastor for eighteen years. I heard once again the words of the emcee and our longtime friend in ministry, Dr. Byron Klaus, as he summed up the evening: "What we have seen here tonight is an Ebenezer. We have created a 'memory stone' to remind you of where you have come from and to say that 'hitherto, God has helped you' and that he will continue to be your help and guide."

I had been searching for an opening thought for a presentation to encourage women's groups to supply funds for "memory bags" for the campers. We would need more than seven hundred memory bags for all the campers by the summer camping season, at a price of $28.67 each.

This was it! Ebenezer.

In 1 Samuel 7 we read of Israel's encounter with the Philistines and Samuel's fervent prayer for God to deliver them from their dreaded enemy. In answer to Samuel's pleadings, God sent thunder and confused the Philistines, routing them throughout the hillsides, giving Israel a lasting victory.

In response to God's action on Israel's behalf, Samuel took a large stone, set it up in the camp, and named it Ebenezer, saying, "Thus far has the Lord helped us" (1 Sam. 7:12). For generations as the people traveled past that stone, it reminded them that in this place God had revealed himself to them and helped them. Samuel created a memorial or a memory stone to remind the Israelites of a place where God had miraculously met them.

When I heard Byron's words on the video, it was as if God said, "This is what you do for the children of Royal Family Kids' Camps for one week out of their year. You are meeting deep needs that they have for genuine love, trust of adults, affirmation, and the knowledge of a God who loves them and will never leave them. They may be hearing it for the very first time in their young lives."

Whenever we think of memory stones or memory bags for the children who come to RFKC camps, we think of Jason Baxter. In 1985 Jason attended our first camp. He was seven years old, and he was the one child the counselors *dreaded* would be assigned to them. He was a disruption to the entire camp. He had been a heroin-addicted baby and as a result was neurologically damaged from birth. He was extremely hyperactive; his foster mother said he chewed his clothes all around the neck and chewed the sleeves all the way up to the elbow. He couldn't learn and was totally unaware of any

world around him. All of his energy was consumed with survival.

When Jason arrived at camp, he discovered that his
brother, from whom he had been separated for two years, was
also at camp. From time to time throughout the day, we
would peer through the window of the nurse's station to see
Jason and his brother sitting with their arms around each
other and watching *Davy & Goliath* videos, just sharing the
joy of being brothers for a week—only to leave and return to
separate foster homes at the end of the week.

The next year when Jason came back to camp, he, along
with the other campers, received a camp duffel bag in which
to take home his belongings. Many of our campers bring
their belongings in a trash bag or a paper grocery sack.

Several years later Jason and his brother were again
together as they flew to Minneapolis for their father's second
wedding. A Royal Family Kids' Camps donor had also flown
to Minneapolis that week to attend the World Series game between the Twins and the Braves.

As he leaned over to place his carry-on bag under the seat,
he noticed a duffel bag with a Royal Family Kids' Camps
logo. Curious to see what the boys had to say about this
camp, he began asking questions.

All the way back to Los Angeles, Jason told him the name
of his counselor for each of the five years he had attended,
what the camp had meant to the brothers while they were separated for the rest of the year, their favorite activities at camp,
and how they missed it now that they were too old to attend.

"I was almost sorry I asked them about camp because they
talked nonstop about it!" our friend reported.

That duffel bag had become a memory stone, an Ebenezer

for Jason Baxter. We wanted each camper to have a memory bag, a keepsake of a life-changing week. The memory bags would contain six items that the campers cherish during the week at camp:

- a Royal Family Kids' Camps T-shirt
- a copy of *The Children's Living Bible,* large print, color-picture edition
- a story-theme workbook
- a photo album of personal photos of their week at camp
- a cassette tape of songs sung during camp
- a camp water bottle sipper

Each sponsoring church tries to provide every camper with two T-shirts, one when they arrive so they are all treated equally and look like their peers, and a second one on Friday morning so they arrive clean and fresh for the foster parents who meet them at the bus. One of these T-shirts is in the memory bag. These T-shirts are more than souvenirs. They are pieces of clothing for children who often come to us with very few clothes in their wardrobe. This is one way we can act on Christ's words in Matthew 25:35-36: "For I was hungry and you gave me something to eat, I was thirsty and you gave me something to drink, I was a stranger and you invited me in, I needed clothes and you clothed me."

As one of our counselors was helping her two campers put their clothes away shortly after arriving at camp, she noticed that one young girl had only two pairs of panties to put away. Thinking that perhaps the girl had left another suitcase or bag on the bus or out in the parking lot, she asked the girl,

"Did you bring any more clothes? I see you have only two pairs of panties for the week."

Her camper answered, "No, this is all I brought. But it will be OK because if I turn them inside out the next day and wash them out the next night, I will have enough for the whole week."

Already at the age of eight, this girl had learned that if she was going to survive in life, she had to learn to take care of herself. Her mother was stoned on drugs and alcohol every morning, and this young girl was already assuming the caretaker responsibilities for the younger children in the home.

Royal Family Kids' Camps ministers to children not only by providing clothing for their bodies but also by providing a Bible for their hearts. For most campers, the Bible they receive in their memory bag is the very first copy of the Scriptures they have ever owned. They ask, "How much will this cost me? These are very expensive. You're going to *give* me this as a gift? What do I have to do for this?"

I wish you could see the faces of some of the campers light up when their counselors underline a Scripture verse that explains the biblical meaning of their name. Imagine the delight when a boy named David or John sees his name in God's book rather than hearing it at the end of a string of curses or four-letter words. Counselors report that some campers experience a deep inner change after they see the value of their personhood in Scripture.

One camper couldn't be persuaded to put the Bible away after discovering that she could read some of the verses and understand them. She was consumed with the joy of having something of her very own and proceeded to carry her Bible around the camp. One counselor found this young girl read-

ing her Bible *at the same time* that she twirled a hula hoop
around her waist.

The third item each camper receives in the memory bag is
a story-theme workbook containing the curriculum to accompany the chapel story for each day of the week. The curriculum exposes children to scriptural role models with whom
they can identify and tells the stories in language unhindered
by Christian jargon.

After the final chapel service, in which graduating campers
were recognized, we talked with twelve-year-old Lizzy, who
was savoring her last day at camp. We asked her, "Lizzy, what
do you remember from your first year of camp?" We hoped
for some great theological lesson that we could hang onto for
courage and motivation to continue developing the Royal
Family Kids' Camps ministry.

First, she remembered all the hot dogs she had eaten. But
then her eyes filled with tears as she said, "What I remember
most is all the workbooks and picture albums you give us
with all the notes from my counselors every year. I had been
saving all mine in a box from every year I had come to camp.
They were very special to me. But when my foster mother
got a new cleaning woman, she got mixed up and threw the
box away. So this year my workbook and picture album will
be really special because now they're the only ones I will have
forever." We try to put together some of the missing pieces of
the campers' childhood, giving them special memories to
carry through life with them.

The fourth item in each memory bag is also used to help
abused and neglected children gain a sense of self-worth.
Most children who come to camp have no visual record of
their lives. When the police come to remove the children

from their home because of family violence, for instance, the last thing the children stop to take with them is their baby album or report cards or baseball-card collection. And even if they would remember to take these valuable memory makers, children in several counties would have these things taken away from them and stored until they would leave the foster-care system maybe ten or fifteen years later, and then only if these items had been moved with the children from foster home to foster home.

Social workers tell us that for most of the children Royal Family Kids' Camps is the *only consistent thing* in their life, the only thing they can count on year after year. They long to come back. Social workers also report that the children bring out their camp photo albums at each of their regular visits, carefully retelling their experiences from camp and naming the camp personnel in each picture.

Because music plays an important role at Royal Family Kids' Camps, we include a fifth item in each memory bag: a tape of the songs the children learn at camp. Most of these children do not come from Christian foster homes or group homes, and much of the music they listen to is anything but good for them.

Donna, a foster mom, told us about Penny, the young camper who lived in her home. Penny was being moved to a new home and was having a difficult time preparing herself for the change that was ahead. Donna said Penny had gone to her room and closed the door. Hoping Penny was all right, Donna stood out in the hall and listened. She heard Penny sing one of the RFKC camp songs over and over. Donna said it was as if the music became a solace for the girl when nothing else seemed to help her pain. We give children a new song to sing, as Psalm 40 states, and the new song brings healing to their soul.

Christ tells us to give a cup of cold water in his name. We take that seriously at Royal Family Kids' Camps. Most of the camps are held in mountainous areas or desert areas. The children's bodies often are underweight, and they easily become dehydrated. The children play and work very hard all week, so we provide campers with a water bottle sipper to make sure they drink water continually throughout the day. This too becomes a reminder of special memories of the week.

One fifty-five-year-old counselor named Paul told us the following story. It was the night before the campers would leave, and the separation factor, as we call it, had set in. Some campers had become withdrawn or sullen, and some of them had become very demonstrative in their behavior; none of them knew how to say good-bye graciously. Their separations had always been hurtful and full of pain, and they knew they must face another separation from someone they had become close to during the week.

As Paul was tucking his two campers into bed, James began to plead with Paul to take him home. Paul was trying to explain to James that he had a job, that he wouldn't be able to spend much time with him, and that he had a family to care for. Paul said to James, "But even though I'm not with you, Jesus will be with you. He will never leave you, James."

James looked up at him with tears in his eyes and said, "Yeah, Paul, but I can't play catch with Jesus. I can play catch with you."

For one week Royal Family Kids' Camps counselors present abused children with a real, lifelike Jesus who can play ball, hold hands, and shoot big-blaster water guns. And this new friend never loses his or her temper, never cusses, even though the child may cuss at him or her. These adults become Jesus walking in flesh and bone, and they leave an indelible impression on children's hearts.

The children can't take their counselors home. But they can take home the tangible items they receive in the memory bag. We are creating memory stones so that one day, many years later, these children will look back at a week at Royal Family Kids' Camps and remember the hope that was rekindled and how their life was changed after that week.

The value of the memory bags became evident to us on Thursday evening, March 14, 1994, when we invited Jason to pray the invocation for our annual fund-raising banquet. Jason was no longer Jason Baxter, who carried the duffel bag on the airplane. Jason had been our first camper to be adopted by a loving, Christian foster mother. He was now Jason Baxter Howell.

Jason had ridden in our car four weeks earlier as we had performed the funeral for a foster brother who died of sudden infant death syndrome. As we rode along, we used the time to ask Jason about his classes and grades at Calvary Chapel Christian High School. Children who come from difficult childhoods need to know they can succeed and that adults are interested in their well-being.

Jason told us of his desire to work in electrical repair someday or in some way work with his hands. But he also left the door open for God to use him in some form of missions work. He is now seventeen years old and studies several hours each evening to keep up his grades. Remember, this is the same Jason who came to camp a hyperactive boy who chewed up his clothes and was unable to learn.

As we listened to Jason that day, we knew we were hearing about a miracle. Jason leaned forward on the edge of the back-seat of our car and said, "Pastor Tesch, you just never know how far God is going to take your idea when you start something like Royal Family Kids' Camps for kids like me."

A few weeks later Jason Baxter Howell prayed this invocation at our banquet:

> Dear Lord, I thank you for this very special gathering of people who care for your children who are so precious in the kingdom of heaven. I thank you that we can gather to recognize what Royal Family Kids' Camps is all about.
>
> Lord, I also thank you for providing such loving counselors that help make these camps possible for your children, children who so very badly need to see your love in practice. Lord, thank you for the very loving environment that Royal Family Kids' Camps has provided for the hurting children. I also ask that you will bring up godly men and women out of the Royal Family Kids' Camps so that they will continue the work that camp planted in their hearts.
>
> I thank you for the difference that this camp has made in my life and for the many memories that I have.
>
> Lord, now I thank you for the food that we are about to eat, and I ask that you bless it to our bodies. In Jesus' name. Amen.

Jason put a memory stone in place for us as he prayed this prayer.

Over six years of attending camp each summer, Jason had

received all the items that are now contained in a memory bag, and he still has many of them today. For Jason and for hundreds of other campers, they are positive memories for a lifetime.

CHAPTER SIX

How Dreams Come True

IN our farewell service from Newport-Mesa Christian Center in 1990, Diane and I recounted the steps God had led us through to arrive at the threshold of beginning Royal Family Kids' Camps, Inc. We talked about the day I came home in July 1990 and told Diane I had decided to resign and develop a full-time ministry for abused children. Diane had thought, *It's either another one of Wayne's "great ideas," or he's going into a midlife crisis.*

Diane was used to my great ideas. Through twenty-seven years of marriage, every week—Diane says sometimes it's every *day*—I have come home excited, saying, "You'll never believe this great idea! I know we can do this!"

Diane often tells me, "Wayne, if you accomplish even one or two of your great ideas in this lifetime, you will be a success." But this time she suspected I was serious. For eighteen years I had been the associate pastor of Newport-Mesa Christian Center, a healthy, thriving church in Southern California. Resigning from the church was a big step.

God had already assured Diane that Royal Family Kids' Camps should become an independent ministry early that summer. It was the last day of camp, Friday afternoon June 29, 1990—the day the children return to their homes. But that year we planned something different.

We had invited all the foster moms and dads and the caretakers of the children to come early to pick them up so that we could put on a program for them. During the course of the week, the children had been learning songs for a musical. For these children, most of whom have short attention spans, it was a major undertaking to learn five songs. But they did it.

We walked into Newport-Mesa Christian Center, where the foster families and caregivers had gathered to pick up their children. The entire choir loft was filled with nearly a hundred young children, each wearing a new white Royal Family Kids' Camps T-shirt and a golden Burger King crown to carry out the Royal Family theme. Diane remembers on that day that God seemed to be speaking to her: "Look at this. This is a glimpse of what eternity will be like if you just keep bringing children to me one at a time."

It's obvious that God brought about his will in our lives through very special circumstances, but this chapter explains that if God has given you a dream—a great idea—he will also give you the means to make it come true. This is our experience, but recognize that God uses many different approaches based on our own personalities and our backgrounds. God uses his Word in places of solitude so that we can hear his voice. God uses circumstances and conflict, role models, and speakers' illustrations. He uses times of worship and supernatural revelations. He places within our souls the direction and desire to follow our Lord and Savior, Jesus Christ. In addition to all this, he places alongside of us significant adults—men and women—to make sure that the gifts and skills developed in us will bring honor and glory to him.

This chapter outlines six steps God used to begin the RFKC ministry to abused and neglected children. Those of you who are familiar with Dr. Robert Schuller's sermon "Ten Building Blocks of a Dream" will see his influence in these thoughts.

Newport-Mesa Christian Center is a church involved in camping ministry. I (Wayne) founded Sonshine Day Camp, a ten-week day camp designed for working parents and children between the ages of seven and twelve. I began Sonshine Kids' Camp, a one-week residence camp for children ages nine to twelve; the camp is held up in the mountains, the great cathedral of the outdoors. There's a ten-week day camp called Young Teen Summer Adventure and a program called Summer Splash for both junior high and high school students. Along with these camps, Royal Family Kids' Camps emerged and has grown from thirty-seven children the first year with only our church participating in 1985 to more than seven hundred children in eighteen camps across the country in 1994.

Why all this emphasis on camping? Children find God at Christian camps. That's where I found God, and there God gave me direction in my life. We wanted to duplicate that model to hundreds of thousands of children. When we arrived at Newport-Mesa Christian Center in 1972, I was given the freedom to develop camps. At the time I had no idea of working with abused and neglected children. But God had a great idea. God was putting Diane and me through the laboratory of life so we could develop the skills and gifts necessary to bring Royal Family Kids' Camps into existence.

That's the first step in how dreams come true: *Dreams that catch our imagination and inspire our wills always begin in the mind of God.* We hadn't planned to launch a camp for abused and neglected children one day in the 1990s, but God had that plan. The dream begins in the mind of God and is imparted to the heart of the dreamer.

The second step is this: *God connects the dream to the dreamer.* Imagine God walking the balcony of heaven, peering over the rail, looking across the earth, looking for men, women, teenagers, boys, and girls to whom he can entrust his dream. He says, "There's one." Then out of his compassion and mind and heart, he plants a seed into a dreamer's mind and heart. He plants it in a man or woman or boy or girl whom he will prepare for the job he has planned for them. Look at Noah, Joseph, Moses, Nehemiah, David, Paul, Deborah. These people are all examples of men and women who were brought to the kingdom with a specific task at a specific time.

Thousands of people accomplish God's will without ever preaching a sermon on Sunday morning. Instead, they preach illustrated life messages every day of the week. They let their pulpit be their executive desk or their workbench in the shop or the teacher's desk in the classroom or the nurse's station at the hospital. Their congregations are their family, their friends, their associates, or their students. They are ordinary people touched by the dreams that God has placed within their hearts.

Where did God connect the dream to me? In an earlier

chapter I referred to a vision the Lord had given me. I believe that vision was God's way of planting his dream in my life. He showed me that vision at three distinct times in my life. The first time I was twelve years old, attending a kids' camp called Lakeview Gospel Camp, near Lake Ontario in upstate New York. It was a Thursday night, a night I will always remember. I was in the Quonset-shaped tabernacle with wooden benches and sawdust for a floor. Kneeling there by myself, I prayed, "Dear God, I'm twelve years old. What am I supposed to do?" A picture came to my mind, a picture of hundreds of thousands of kids, a sea full of faces that were African-American, Caucasian, Hispanic, and Asian.

When my mom picked me up on Saturday, she asked what happened at camp. I announced, "Mom, God has called me to be a youth pastor and work with kids. I'm moving to California because I'm going to be a preacher."

I still chuckle at my mom's response: "Dear God. Not another preacher in the family." She knew all too well the financial hardship of ministers in fledgling churches.

The second time I saw the picture, I was twenty-four years old. Diane and I had just moved from New York, and I had set up my office at Newport-Mesa Christian Center. The office was a classroom with an eight-foot table and a folding chair. I was sitting in my chair in the new office, looking at the back wall, and again I prayed, "Here I am at a new position, Lord. What do you want me to do?" It was as if God put a slide in a projector and flashed up on the wall the picture I had seen when I was twelve years old, with hundreds of faces projected on the bare wall. I decided that I had better get started, and I set out to form ministries for our church's children.

The third time God connected the dream to the dreamer was in 1985, when I was thirty-six years old. I was in the chapel at the campground where we held the very first RFKC camp. As I looked over the pews on Thursday evening, I saw a microcosm of the dream that God had given me when I was twelve years old. But this time what I saw was not a dream; it was reality. There were African-American, Caucasian, Hispanic, and Asian children staring up at me. All of a sudden the dream was living and breathing. I knew that it was more than just my dream; it was God who had prepared that time and that place. God connected the dream with the dreamer.

The third step in the fulfillment of the dream is this: *The dream alters your schedule.* The dream enters a gestation period. God has given the dream a life of its own, and it becomes all-consuming. That's the way it is with the dream that God imparts from his heart to your heart. You begin to study. You begin to pray. You begin to find information. You write. You read. You become involved in developing strategies to accomplish the dream. You act on plans to make the dream a reality. You reach out, and you begin to feel the pain within your heart. You begin to sense the hurt of the people you're helping. You go through an incredible experience in order to see the dream fulfilled. For Diane and me, this has begun to occur over the past ten years since the inception of Royal Family Kids' Camps.

I was doing more to develop the dream because it continued to demand more and more of my time. The gestation period strains the patience of the dreamer waiting for the birth of the dream. I began to ask God, "Why can't it happen right now? Why is it taking so long? Will I ever live to see the dream fulfilled?"

While the dreamer waits, the rhythm beats, *Plod on. Plod on. Plod on.* It is patience that identifies those who fulfill the divine dream. Impatient dreamers look for shortcuts and cheap discounts on the price of being faithful. Impatient dreamers will discover that in choosing the painless, easy road, they are in fact walking down the path of shame, boredom, and failure. The dreamer must realize that it takes time—sometimes years—to develop the dream God has imparted.

Christ knew at the age of twelve that he had a mission to accomplish in his lifetime. At age thirty he finally began the mission. David was crowned king when he was thirty years old. David never built the temple he dreamed of building, but his son Solomon accomplished what David desired.

Your dream may take time to develop. Be patient, for God is working out the plans for you. "'I know the plans I have for you,' declares the Lord, 'plans to prosper you and not to harm you, plans to give you hope and a future'" (Jer. 29:11).

While you wait, plan, and plod on, enjoy the wonderment of asking, What will happen? Remember that all the while, God is already at work on the next step. Be "confident of this, that he who began a good work in you will carry it on to completion," we are told in Philippians 1:6.

Step four in watching the dream come true is this: *Support comes from unexpected sources.* The dream that originated in the mind of God and was planted in the heart of the dreamer is like a magnet that draws the right people at the right time. God provides the right counsel to the right people to help along the way. It was in 1986 that our camp grandpa and grandma, the McNutts, said with tears in their eyes, "Wayne, other churches need to do this." But in order to have the dream, to multiply this program, the entire structural organization had to change. No longer could I be the camp director. Instead, God had already placed his hand on the shoulder of the next director. He was being prepared to handle that responsibility. God brought the right people at the right time. I handed off the baton to my successor so the dream could continue to the next stage of development.

Since then, of course, I have placed the dream into the hands not only of many camp directors who come for training with us but also of local churches who want to reach out to the children. These camp directors and counselors in turn give up a week of vacation and innumerable hours for preparation to make Royal Family Kids' Camps a special week in the life of needy children.

Remember, if it is God's dream, he will bring the right people at the right time. And these people will be dear to you. We have friends who go with us to ball games, who pray with us, who go to lunch with us. We have friends who hold us accountable in our spiritual lives. But we have no more exhilarating relationship than with the friends who have ministered alongside us to advance and accomplish God's dream. God brought people who are willing to risk and learn, to pray and hurt, to see the pain of children and administer the medicine of God's love. Counselors, staff members, prayer partners, donors—they all come from unexpected sources. Only the hand of God moves people to become involved.

Following our fourth year of camp in Southern California, we became frustrated that we weren't doing more to impact abused children in our county. After we shared this frustration with the camp grandma, Marita McNutt, she asked us a most obvious question: "Why don't you involve additional churches to duplicate what you are already doing?"

Although this was the obvious way to impact more children's lives, when I (Diane) heard the word *duplicate,* my mind went back to my earlier days of working in fast-food franchising, and I knew what that entailed. But it was as if a bolt of lightning hit both Wayne and me at the same time. We knew we had to record everything we had done in one location, refine the process so it would be foolproof, document everything, and train others to do it the same way in other locations.

My employer, a commercial real-estate developer, had visited the camp for a few hours one afternoon that same week. When I returned to work the following Monday, he called me into his office and made a proposal.

He asked a few questions about our future plans for Royal Family Kids' Camps and added that he could sense our frustration at not being able to take it to a higher level of development than one camp. He indicated that he could give me three months off because a project I had been working on was awaiting permit approval. I could use those months to write the training and operations manuals we would need to train other camp directors to duplicate the camp model. Then he told me it would be *paid* time off, using funds from a future bonus incentive tied to the project I was working on. To someone who likes to write and to document procedures, it felt as if someone had laid a gold brick in my hands.

Those manuals are still in use and in revision today in training new camp directors. Help had come from an unexpected source.

In November 1990, two months after we left the position

at the church to launch Royal Family Kids' Camps, Inc. as a full-time ministry, the first big test of our faith came. The engine on one of our cars became totally disabled on the freeway one evening as Wayne returned from a speaking engagement. We had asked God to give us one or two more years with our cars so we could avoid a car payment during our first two years away from the church. But God had a plan to teach us faith and strengthen our belief that he really wanted this ministry to continue.

We had been praying for a vehicle and had priced a van but had determined it was out of the question. In January a businessman invited us to dinner and presented us with a set of keys to an Astro van. Not just any vehicle, but a *van!* It was a perfect vehicle for our needs in this growing organization. An unexpected source had supplied us with a vehicle.

Our first offices were in the two spare bedrooms of our home, and our warehouse was the garage. After three years we needed to add an additional office person. The two bedrooms were a bit more provincial than the image we wanted to portray, and we definitely had no room for a third person in our "offices."

By November 1992 we began to pray about office space, and a board member suggested that many nonprofit organizations are given space in vacant office buildings. This seemed to us like something that happened only to other people.

In February 1993 a phone call came from a longtime friend who believed in the ministry to abused children. He told us he had rented a warehouse with two offices in front, but he didn't need the offices and all the warehouse space. He offered to donate the space to us and invited us to come look at it. After looking it over, we assured him it would move us beyond our humble beginnings in the back two bedrooms of our home. We eagerly accepted his offer. The building was painted white with purple trim—the Royal Family Kids' Camps colors! How could this be? It looked as if we had planned it that way.

Now we had offices and warehouse space, but we had no shelving to store everything in this big open warehouse. We left the meeting at the offices, and I (Wayne) went on to meet with another friend who owned a manufacturing business. While waiting for the owner to join me for lunch, I asked the secretary where we might purchase shelving. She showed me their newly designed warehouse and offered to give me four pallets of metal shelves they had just removed from their old warehouse.

In less than an hour we had offices, a warehouse, and shelving to fill it—with extra shelves left over. Again, God had moved people, and help had come from unexpected sources.

In March 1993 God brought into our lives another person who was moved by the needs of abused and neglected children. He was instrumental in securing a substantial grant that would take off some of the financial pressure that is so much a part of a young, rapidly growing organization. We realized later that he had become the "angel" that one of our friends had prayed for on the eve of our farewell from Newport-Mesa Christian Center in 1990. Again, help came from an unexpected source. And it continues to come, week after week, from faithful friends who give and who pray.

The fifth step in making dreams come true is this: *The dreamer has setbacks and frustrations.* We can look through Scripture and see the life of Paul and Moses. When it comes to setbacks, they had their share. So did Joseph. The dreamer

must understand that setbacks and frustrations, misunder-
standing and ridicule will always be part of the process. But
experience teaches the dreamer to embrace the opposition
and find in the middle of the frustration a principle: God is
using the opposition to further the dream. This step begins to
mature the dreamer. It forces the dreamer to focus on the
dream and not on the circumstances.

Through all this, we reach the sixth step: *The dreamer is
changed by the dream.* I am not the person I was in 1972,
beginning the first Sonshine Kids' Camp for the Christian
children of Newport-Mesa Christian Center. My heart and
life have changed as a result of moving with God. God has
changed my heart and opened my mind to the cries of the
unfortunate children who have been made victims by adults.
More than 3 million children are abused and neglected
because adults use power instead of love. One woman in
three is molested. One in six men is molested, beaten,
abused, or neglected. Those lives can be destroyed by abuse,
or they can be redeemed by love. That's what we do at Royal
Family Kids' Camps.

Several years ago Diane and I had been driving for nine
hours when we reached Prescott, Arizona, the site of Arizona's
first RFKC camp, with twenty-seven children. We had gotten
lost going through the mountains, and we finally thought we
had found the camp. We turned onto a dirt road, not really
sure where we were. There ahead of us we saw a woman with
two young girls, one on her right and one on her left, each
one holding her hand. Diane said, "That's our sign: one adult
for every two children. It's becoming a hallmark of Royal
Family Kids' Camps." We both looked at each other with tear-
filled eyes as we realized the dream had been duplicated in yet

a third location, and our lives were being changed and guided more and more by the dream. The dream continued to change us as it became more evident to us that this was more than a simple ministry led by two people.

And the dream continues to change us every day. I asked a young boy at the camp how he felt about the week, and without hesitating he looked up and said, "This must be what heaven is like." Hearing responses like that changes me. It makes me want all the more to provide a safe harbor for children battling the waves, winds, and storms of life.

God is still walking the balcony of heaven, looking across this earth to find people in whom he can plant his dream. Royal Family Kids' Camps was the dream he gave to Diane and me. And we hope and pray that the dream he gives you might be to reach out to abused and neglected children too, either through Royal Family Kids' Camps or through some other means.

Dreams become reality. Never doubt it.

TWO

How to Turn the Key:
Practical Help for Victims
of Child Abuse

The Church: A Roadblock or a Resource?

In the previous pages you have walked with Wayne and Diane Tesch through the exciting development and expansion of Royal Family Kids' Camps. But Wayne and Diane's concerns reach farther than their own ministry, as exciting and healing as it is.

They are also eager to see believers and pastors, indeed the entire body of Christ, learn more about the tragedy of child abuse and neglect. They want to see Christians become a vital resource in ministry to this need. They long to see the Lord's people fulfill the assurance of the psalmist as applied to abused and neglected children: "When my father and my mother forsake me, then the Lord will take care of me" (Ps. 27:10, NKJV).

I first met Wayne Tesch in the coffee shop of the San Diego Airport. As I ate marginal airport food for which I had paid "captive audience" price, I was paying no attention to either the food or the price. I was experiencing one of those spiritually charged times as I shared the meal with this unassuming yet dynamic Christian man whom I had just met.

In our work my wife, Anne, and I travel across the country educating religious leaders on crime-victim issues, seeking to identify and encourage faith-based victim-assistance programs and ministries. Thus it was that I found myself on this day in this busy airport terminal with this remarkable person.

Wayne had agreed to accommodate my schedule and meet in this transient arena to share the story that had touched my heart and Anne's more profoundly than has any other victim-assistance venture we know.

It has been said that unless you are prepared both to have your heart broken and to be moved to action, do not have lunch with Wayne Tesch. I bear personal testimony to that statement.

I liked what I heard Tesch say about mobilizing the church to respond to the needs of abused children. For too long the church has been a roadblock instead of a resource. We deny the reality of child abuse: "It doesn't happen in my congregation." We can be defensive: "I don't want anyone to know what has occurred in my Christian home or church." We sometimes assist the offender at the expense of the victim; this is particularly true if the abuser is active in the church. We can even blame the child victim for "not being obedient" or for being "seductive."

However, the church is increasingly becoming a valued resource. The next chapters of this book will outline ways you can elevate ministry to abused and neglected children to an important mission for God's people. The prophet Jeremiah lamented, "For the wound of the daughter of my people is my heart wounded. . . . Is there no balm in Gilead? Is there no physician there?" (Jer. 8:21-22, RSV).

The following chapters say yes, there is a balm in the Gilead of abused and neglected children as the body of Christ becomes their healing agent. As you read the challenges for individual Christians, pastors, and the church as a whole to become involved in healing the scars of wounded children,

open your heart to learn how God may want to use the gifts
he has given you.

REV. DAVID W. DELAPLANE
Executive Director, The Spiritual Dimension in Victim Services

CHAPTER SEVEN

Sexual Abuse of Children: The Best-Kept Secret of the Secret World

LIBBY AND RIKKI were twin girls, alike in almost every way. What made their father decide that Libby would be the object of his sexual advances? We'll never know because their father is dead now. Libby and Rikki came home one day from playing down the street, but their parents didn't answer their calls when they came into the house. Searching through their home, the twins discovered the corpses of their parents, victims of an apparent suicide pact.

The girls were fortunate enough to be placed together in a loving Christian foster home, but Libby wouldn't let her new foster father near her. She remembered too well what happened if an adult man got too close. She wouldn't hug her foster father, wouldn't let him hold her, wouldn't display any physical affection. It was a long time before Libby could trust a grown man, a long time before her fragile confidence could be restored.

Child sexual abuse is an insidious form of abuse that is felt with more shame and treated with more secrecy than any other form of abuse. It is perpetrated by family members, as in Libby's case, and also by pedophiles and child molesters who are not part of the victim's family but who may be close friends of the family.

The scope of child sexual abuse, whether in the home or perpetrated by strangers, is incredible. Some estimates indicate that one in ten families in the U.S. is involved in sexual abuse.[1] The average victim is eleven years old, although children still in infancy have been abused. Although in the case of incest the incident is sometimes one isolated act, it is more commonly a pattern that can last up to five years or longer.[2] Sexual abuse is one of the top three reasons that children run away from home.[3]

One recent study focusing on adult female rape victims found that nearly 30 percent admitted to having been raped before they were ten years old. More than 30 percent were raped when they were between the ages of eleven and seventeen.[4] In spite of the apparent widespread occurrence of child sexual abuse, it is probably the most unreported form of abuse—for a variety of reasons. In the first place, societal taboos foster denial and nonrecognition. Also, a child who has been sexually abused frequently will not exhibit the outward signs that expose other forms of abuse. Finally, sexual abusers of children are the ones who go to the greatest lengths to assure that this is "our secret"; therefore, victims of child sexual abuse are least likely and least able to report what has happened.[5]

Because many incidents go unreported, complete information on child sexual abuse and abusers is not available, but the best research shows several facts about this crisis:

- Victims of child sexual abuse are usually not "attacked" by a stranger. Generally the perpetrator is well known to them: a parent, a relative, or a family friend. Studies show that 75 percent to 85 percent of reported sexual abusers say they knew their victim before the first incidence of abuse.
- Child sexual abuse perpetrated by someone known to the child usually is conducted in the home of the victim or the abuser.
- Child sexual abuse perpetrated by a stranger usually is conducted outdoors in warm weather.
- In many cases coercion is not required in order to molest a child. Rather the perpetrator has won the trust of the child through affection or gifts, and the child allows the molestation without protest.
- Although in cases of pedophilia, as opposed to incest, most of the victims are boys abused by men, most child molesters say their adult sexual orientation is heterosexual.
- The majority of known child sexual abusers are men.
- Girls are the most frequent victims of child sexual abuse.[6]
- Although some people believe that only very attractive or "seductive" children are at risk or that molestation happens only to children in "bad" neighborhoods or children who are improperly supervised, sexual abuse may happen to children of any age, whether beautiful or plain, whether they live in good or bad neighbor-

hoods, whether they are properly supervised or terribly neglected.[7]

Incest

Studies show that about 50 percent of all reported child sexual abuse cases involve incest.[8] However, because intrafamilial child sexual abuse is the least likely kind to be reported, this figure is probably very understated. The most common form of incest is between father or stepfather and daughter. About seven of eight reported cases of incest involve young girls rather than young boys.[9] The perpetrator is not always someone who "looks" like a child molester or who obviously drinks too much; the person can be a church leader or an astute businessperson.

A variety of reasons have been suggested for why some men sexually use their daughters or stepdaughters. As with most abusive parents, sexual abusers often were physically and/or sexually abused as children.[10] They may also feel insecure with themselves and their ability to handle the stresses of marriage and fatherhood. A father who feels this way may respond in one of two directions: rigid authoritarianism or passive dependency. In either case, incest may result.[11] The authoritarian type will feel more in charge if he can subjugate his daughter sexually. The dependent type will substitute the easy target of his daughter for a normal sexual relationship with his wife, demanding that his needs be met as if he were the child.

Another contributing factor to the onset of incest between father or stepfather and daughter can include the daughter's role as the central female of the house when the mother is absent or not able or willing to assume this role.[12] The daughter then may be seen as the "little mother" of the household and is open to abuse by the father or stepfather who places her in the role of his "little wife."

In some cases the wife and mother may be aware of the incest but is unable or unwilling to stop it. In such a case the mother may see her daughter as a rival for her husband rather than as the abused victim of a sick person. If you are a mother who suspects or has reason to suspect that your husband or male friend may be abusing your daughter, you *must* do two things:

1. Find out. If you're ignoring telltale evidence because you're certain that your husband or friend would *never* do that, then you may be allowing the child you love to suffer terribly. Ask your daughter or confront your husband or the friend. If you are mistaken, you'll be relieved. But if you are correct, you must report the abuse and save your child.

2. If your husband or friend admits the abuse but is remorseful and promises that it will never happen again, *don't believe him.* Your caution has nothing to do with your love for him and everything to do with protecting your child. Report the abuse to the proper authorities, and insist that the offender see a counselor who can advise you whether or not the man can remain in your home and keep his promise not to touch your daughter. In the meantime do not allow him to be alone with your children, even for a minute. If the counselor determines that your husband or male friend will abuse again, then he must go live

somewhere else while he undergoes therapy and over-comes this problem.

It is very important for your daughter's self-esteem to remove the offender rather than your daughter from your home. Make your daughter understand that what happened to her was not her fault. It was the abuser's fault, and he has to leave until he is better. If you send your daughter away, not only will she feel that she is being punished and internalize the blame for this incident, but your abusing spouse or friend probably will turn his attention to other children in the home.

Other types of incest, including father-son, mother-son, mother-daughter, and sibling incest are not nearly as com-mon as father-daughter, so less research has been devoted to them. However, any child sexual abuse has the potential for profoundly devastating the child as well as the family.

Pedophilia

In the longest and costliest criminal trial ever conducted in North Carolina, one man was convicted of ninety-nine counts of rape and other crimes against children. One hundred forty-eight counts against the same man had been dropped before the trial. He had been the owner of a day-care center. The children's parents had *entrusted* their children to him and his staff.[13]

Child sexual abuse such as this, which is perpetrated out-side the family, is often the work of a pedophile, someone whose sexual orientation is directed toward children. Pedo-philes prefer children as the objects of their sexual gratifica-tion. These are the "stranger danger" people we warn our children about, but it may not always be a stranger who threatens our children, as the North Carolina incident illustrates. What can you know about pedophiles, and how can you protect your children from them?

Most pedophiles are men. Although females can be pedophiles, it is very rare. Pedophiles plan their lifestyle to gain access to children. They may even marry in order to get close to the children of their new spouse. They are often the "special friend" of the children they abuse. For instance, they may give the children presents, take them on outings, or invite them home with them. Pedophiles may invest weeks in grooming their intended victims, gaining their confidence. Pedophiles may also use pornography or child pornography to desensitize the intended victims, showing them that other children do these things and enjoy them.

Pornography plays different roles in child sexual abuse. Many pedophiles use pornography to teach victims how to perform sexual acts. Others take pictures or videos of their victims not only for personal pleasure but also for trade with other pedophiles. Photographs and videos may also be used to blackmail victims; the abuser may threaten to show the bad pictures to parents or to have them published in the newspaper if the children tell what has happened to them.

Pedophiles themselves claim that 20 million American men are sexually attracted only to boys.[14] These pedophiles will prey on prepubescent boys who have no father figure or adult-male role model. The affection and attention of a pedophile, lavished on a lonely young boy, serve to break down any barriers the boy may have, opening him to the sexual suggestions of the pedophile. Many adult male pedophiles see the Greek tradition of pederasty as a good one and are working to make sex between men and boys legal and accepted in our society through such organizations as the North American Man-Boy Love Association.

Adolescent Offenders

Recent news reports tell haunting stories of teenage baby-sitters who turned out to be child abusers, sometimes sexually abusing the children for whom they were caring. But it is actually not surprising when you consider that studies of adult sex offenders show that their problems began when they were young. Some child molesters committed their first sex offense when they were as young as eight years old; some rapists committed their first rape when they were only nine years old. Another study found that about 35 percent of adult sex offenders had already begun to exhibit behaviors such as exhibitionism and voyeurism when they were adolescents.[15]

In the past, adolescents who exhibited inappropriate sexual behavior with other children were generally regarded as merely exploring their emerging sexuality. However, the most recent research shows that juvenile offenders are representing a larger and larger proportion of all sex crimes. Add to this the fact that inappropriate sexual behavior in adolescents seems to precede adult sex offenses, and the problem of juveniles abusing juveniles appears to be a major issue.[16]

Most adolescent sex offenders are male, although female adolescents can also be sex abusers. In their book *Helping Victims of Sexual Abuse,* Lynn Heitritter and Jeanette Vought give an idea of how an adolescent offender may find the opportunity to develop and maintain a sexual relationship with a much younger child:

He is typically a nice quiet young man, a loner who

keeps to himself. He is usually an average or above average student who is appreciated by his teachers because of his pleasing behavior. He is usually isolated from peers, has a low self-esteem, and a history of abuse, usually sexual. Because he does not have friends who take up his time and because he is quiet and well behaved, he is often asked to babysit for small children. His victims are usually fond of him and will participate in sexual activities for long periods of time before the secret about the abuse comes out. If the children do tell about the abuse, they may not be believed, because he is such a "nice guy."[17]

On the opposite side of the coin, some juvenile offenders may use violence and force to abuse children sexually. These offenders often have been violently abused themselves and are trying to regain some control in their lives by overpowering and controlling someone weaker. They also may have a desire to express pent-up anger and to humiliate someone in the same way they have been humiliated.

Children are just as devastated by an adolescent abuser as they are by an adult sexual abuser. If you are concerned about protecting your children from abuse by adolescents, do not allow an adolescent male to baby-sit for your children. Although this sounds discriminatory, it only makes sense when research shows that most child sexual abuse is perpetrated by males.

Ongoing Sexual Abuse

In many reported cases children are sexually abused not in one isolated incident but on a continuing basis. The ongoing relationship of abuser and abused moves through several stages:

1. *Engagement:* The abuser gains the child's trust and cooperation through nonthreatening, nonforcible means, such as games.
2. *Sexual interaction:* Sexual activity such as fondling is introduced, but these activities generally build in intimacy and frequency.
3. *Secrecy:* The child has been engaged in sexual activity, and secrecy is enforced so the perpetrator will not be caught and can continue to abuse the child.
4. *Accidental or purposeful disclosure:* This step may never be reached because a child victim is often afraid to report the abuse or accepts it as the price of affection and affirmation. Accidental disclosure implies that the abuse has been discovered before either party was ready for disclosure and may precipitate a crisis. Because the victim only then unwillingly discloses the abuse, he or she may not be believed. Unless a child victim receives immediate support after disclosure, the victim will frequently retract and say the story was a lie. Tragically, family members are more willing to believe that a child has lied than that a child was abused.
5. *Suppression:* Families have a tendency to suppress any publicity or information surrounding the circumstances of child sexual abuse once the disclosure stage has been reached, especially if the abuser is a family member of the victim. The victim may even be

forced to recant the disclosure or state that the consequences were minimal—"no harm done."

Child victims of sexual abuse generally feel unable to stop
the abuse, especially because the abuser is stronger and older.
The victims are forced to "accept" what is happening because
they are helpless to stop it. Once victims feel forced to accept
the situation, they may also mentally assume the blame for
what is happening. Alcoholism, drug abuse, and self-destructive behavior have all been identified as "accommodation
mechanisms" developed to help child victims cope with continued sexual abuse.[18]

Effects of Sexual Abuse

The long-lasting effects of sexual abuse of children are
very similar to the scars suffered by a child abused in any
way: loss of trust, anger, fear, and feelings of helplessness.

Victims of child sexual abuse may be more likely to blame
themselves and suffer with guilt than would children abused
in any other way, in part because society regards sexually
abused children differently than any other abused children.
Because victims of child sexual abuse are at a physical disad-
vantage and are in no position to fight back against an adult
perpetrator, they may be forced to accept what is happening.
This acceptance is sometimes mistaken for consent. Some
people blame young female victims of sexual abuse for the
abuse because their clothes or their actions were considered to
be seductive.

However, long-lasting effects of child sexual abuse can be
mitigated. Prognosis for a victim's recovery is especially good if

1. *The child is not blamed for the abuse.* If your child is sexually abused, never make him or her feel responsible. Establish right away that all the guilt lies on the abusive adult.
2. *The child receives the support and protection of family.* It's very important that whether or not the abuser is a family member, the rest of the family members rally around the victim and make him or her feel safe and secure.
3. *Consequences to the family are minimal.* Child sexual abuse—like any other form of child abuse—must be reported to the authorities when it is discovered, even if the incident occurs within the family. The victim is likely to recover best from the incident if disclosure doesn't disrupt family life violently.
4. *The family is not dysfunctional.* A healthy home and family life will help the victim of child sexual abuse recover more readily.
5. *The victim was stable emotionally before the abuse began.* An emotionally healthy child will recover better from the serious effects of sexual abuse than a child who was troubled to begin with.[19]

The sexually abused child has the best possible chance for recovery if all of these conditions are met. Note that some of the conditions need to be met beforehand: providing a stable home and family environment for your child and insuring that your child is emotionally healthy. These steps will also help to create an environment in which your child feels free to talk to you, helping the child to tell you about a potential abuse situation and perhaps avert a tragedy before it happens.

Later chapters will discuss steps parents can take to protect their children from sexual abuse as well as steps pastors and Christian counselors can take to help victims of child sexual abuse.

CHAPTER EIGHT

Rebuilding the Wall: A Model for the Church's Response

EVEN before Clint and Scott were taken away from their parents, Clint would take Scott to Sunday school. Their mom and dad, who were heavy drug users, often were violent with each other as well as with their young sons. But Clint was smart enough to know that they were safe from their parents, and safe from abuse, when they went to church. So every Sunday morning seven-year-old Clint helped five-year-old Scott get dressed so that they could go to Sunday school.

Sunday school couldn't save them from the neglect and abuse they suffered at home. When their dad went to jail, Scott and Clint went into foster care. They were lucky enough to be placed in a foster home together. And better yet, Clint discovered that his foster parents went to church! He and Scott would still be able to go to Sunday school. Soon Clint even made a public profession of faith in Jesus.

One day Clint's social worker took him to visit his father in prison. That afternoon the social worker told Clint's foster mother, "You would have been so proud of Clint this afternoon. Talking to his dad on the prison telephone, through the plateglass window, he explained God's plan to him. Clint told his father that only God could help him and change him."

Clint's Christian witness didn't stop there either. When he decided to be baptized, his foster mother invited his natural mother to attend the service. As Clint's natural mother watched the baptism, she said to the foster mother, "This is the first time I've ever been in church." The first time she was in church, she heard her own son share the testimony of God's love.

God loves children, and he is not shy to let us know that we ought to love our children too. "Behold, children are a heritage from the Lord, the fruit of the womb is a reward. Like arrows in the hand of a warrior, so are the children of one's youth. Happy is the man who has his quiver full of them" (Ps. 127:3-5, NKJV).

The Christian church wields an awesome power to heal the scars of child abuse and even to help put back together families that have been broken by it. What is the church's best response to the secret world of child abuse?

The New Mission Field

If your church is like the one we attend, you're helping to support missionaries to a variety of mission fields, not simply foreign missions and home missions as in the past, but numerous special missions as well. These include ministries to handicapped people, to people in the inner city, to substance abusers, to various ethnic groups, to the military, to unwed mothers, to prisoners, and to many others. Each of these ministries is involved in good work for people who desperately need the help.

Let us suggest another important mission field: abused and neglected children. Nearly 3 million American children were reported as abused or neglected in 1993. That is a mission field of 3 million people whom God prizes. God loves children, and he wants us to be his hands and feet and arms to reach abused and neglected children. Jesus said the angels of children constantly behold the face of the Father (Matt. 18:10). I suggest that the very first way the Christian church can begin addressing the problems of child abuse in America is to recognize that the abused children are a mission field in need of missionaries. We send missionaries all over the world. Let's send them into the secret world of abused children.

A model for how to shape an effective mission to abused children of our land can be taken from the Old Testament story of Nehemiah, who rebuilt the wall around Jerusalem after the Israelites returned from captivity. Just as Nehemiah led the people in restoring their fragmented and bruised nation, the church can restore hope and life to the fragmented and bruised lives of abused and neglected children.

Let's examine several steps Nehemiah took in rebuilding the wall. The first step Nehemiah took when he felt God's call to rebuild the wall was to understand the extent of the problem.

1. Understand the problem

"One of my brothers came from Judah with some other men," Nehemiah writes, "and I questioned them about the

Jewish remnant that survived the exile" (Neh. 1:2). Nehemiah wanted to get all the information he could about the task he felt called to undertake.

Similarly, when the church decides to reach out to abused children, we must understand the problem as fully as we possibly can. The church must educate Christians on the issue of child abuse. For too long the information has remained in the secret world of the abused; it's time to bring it into the open. Sometimes the information will be harsh and brutal, but we must not run from the facts or the people behind them just because we are uncomfortable with the graphic details. Graphic stories are the norm for abused children. For 3 million kids, physical and sexual abuse and neglect are everyday experiences. Christians can show these children that abuse doesn't have to be "normal": Normal childhood should include security, happiness, and the opportunity to rebuild a life broken by abuse or neglect. But we Christians can't help abused children until we understand the facts and support the ministries that currently help abused children. Churches must challenge people to become involved as volunteers or as donors in helping children bruised by emotional and physical abuse.

Not only must the church educate its people about child abuse as an issue but it also must safeguard its own children against potential abuse. The church can do that in three ways. First, it can teach body-safety classes aimed at helping children know the difference between good and bad touching as well as helping them know how to protect themselves from molestation. Second, the church can screen people who will be working with children in an attempt to identify potential abusers. Third, the church can implement a team-teaching approach in its children's programs. All classes and outings should be arranged so that a minimum of two adults are always present, preferably with one or more of the children's parents in attendance. Appendix C lists several valuable resources churches can use to help prevent child abuse in their church.

2. Respond with prayer

After Nehemiah hears the report about the condition of the wall around Jerusalem, he responds with grief and prayer. "When I heard these things, I sat down and wept. For some days I mourned and fasted and prayed before the God of heaven" (Neh.1:4). Nehemiah passionately prays to God, asking for his help in rebuilding the wall and restoring God's people to their former status.

Similarly, the church must respond in prayer to the plight of abused children. The Bible continually reminds us that all great works begin with prayer. The great work of mending the hearts and lives of abused children also will require honest, fervent prayer. Christ himself models this for us. "Then little children were brought to Jesus for him to place his hands on them and pray for them. But the disciples rebuked those who brought them. Jesus said, 'Let the little children come to me, and do not hinder them, for the kingdom of heaven belongs to such as these'" (Matt. 19:13-14).

I (Wayne) can remember arriving at one of our camps during the afternoon and seeing the campers and counselors swimming and playing in the pool to beat the heat. I saw one shivering young boy cross the deck to Mary, one of our camp staff members. Mary wrapped the little guy up in a fluffy San Diego Padres beach towel and sat him on her lap. As I watched, I saw the child nestle into Mary's arms, and I saw her eyes close. Mary was praying for the young boy. He found in that young woman's arms the love of Christ. The young boy found not only someone to cuddle him but also someone to give him God's blessings.

You may or may not be in a position to put your hands on the heads of abused children and pray for them, but every Christian in America can remember these kids in their prayers once a day. That in itself will make the heart of the church sensitive to the needs of the children.

In the New Testament we see Christ's heart broken with compassion for a widow whose only son had died: "As he approached the town gate, a dead person was being carried out—the only son of his mother, and she was a widow. And a large crowd from the town was with her. When the Lord saw her, his heart went out to her and he said, 'Don't cry'" (Luke 7:12-13). Christ's heart went out to her. His compassion led him to raise the widow's son from death. Our hearts go out to neglected and abused children. We can allow that compassion to motivate us to work to raise them from their emotional death and physical pain.

3. Plan the work

When God called Nehemiah to rebuild the wall around Jerusalem, he also called him to plan how that rebuilding would be done. As it happened, Nehemiah was the cupbearer of the ruler Artaxerxes. Nehemiah needed Artaxerxes' permission to rebuild the wall. Because Nehemiah believed so strongly that God would soften Artaxerxes' heart, he boldly planned out his needs before he even went to ask for the king's permission. When Nehemiah approached the king, he already had a plan.

The church also must plan how to address the problems of child abuse. The following chapters of this book outline several plans for how the church can best respond to the crisis of child abuse. As you and your church make your plan, use one of the suggested plans or modify it to meet the needs of your church and community.

4. Pull together

The rebuilding of the wall around Jerusalem is really a tale of cooperative effort. A glance at Nehemiah 3 reads like a *Who's Who* of old Jerusalem inhabitants. Everyone worked together; everyone labored side by side. "Eliashib the high priest and his fellow priests went to work. . . . The men of Jericho built the adjoining section, and Zaccur son of Imri built next to them. . . . Meremoth son of Uriah, the son of Hakkoz, repaired the next section. Next to him Meshullam . . . made repairs, and next to him Zadok son of Baana" (Neh. 3:1-4).

The entire chapter lists all the different people who worked together to rebuild the wall. It serves as a perfect model for outreach to abused children. People from all backgrounds and life experiences can have a strong impact when they work together for God.

I'm reminded of Craig, a volunteer counselor at an RFKC camp in Arizona. Because our camps have a ratio of one counselor to every two campers, each camper gets a lot of concentrated affirmation and support from a counselor. Craig had grown particularly close to one of the boys, Ricky, and he wanted to keep up contact even after camp had ended. Craig's wife, Lucy, however, was reluctant. After all, she and

Craig were not foster parents; they weren't psychologists; they weren't trained social workers. What could they possibly offer an abused child who had been removed from his home? Lucy doubted whether they had the skills, time, or resources to help anyone.

But Craig persisted, believing they could make a difference in this young boy's life. He and Lucy received the county's permission to continue to see Ricky and to take him on special outings. The opportunity to see and spend time with Craig overjoyed Ricky, who had never had such healthy, wholesome attention from an adult. On one outing Craig noticed that Ricky's shoes were falling apart. The next time he saw Ricky, Lucy had agreed to come along. Together they bought Ricky some new tennis shoes. When Craig and Lucy saw Ricky again, he gratefully said, "I just want to thank you for those new shoes you bought me."

Lucy became a believer that day. Yes, Ricky needed foster parenting, a social worker, maybe even therapy with a psychologist. But he also needed the help of loving friends. Lucy realized that anyone who is willing to give a simple gesture of love or a small gift like new shoes can make a real difference to a kid like Ricky. "Craig, we raised three children," she reflected later, "and I don't think any of them ever thanked us for new shoes."

Working together, we can change the lives of neglected and abused children.

5. Face the challenge

Nehemiah knew that he was doing God's work as he rebuilt the wall around Jerusalem, but this did not mean that he did not have adversaries, setbacks, and problems. His response to these challenges was simply to *face* them.

As the church works to save abused children and help put their lives back together, it will encounter problems as well. One big problem we encountered at Royal Family Kids' Camps was named Stevie. Stevie first came to camp when he was just seven years old. His counselor, Larry, who had a full-time job at a home for boys, felt prepared for anything. But that was before Larry actually met Stevie.

When Stevie arrived at camp, he staked out the top bunk for himself. When Larry came into the room to talk with Stevie, he walked up to the bed, found Stevie in the bunk, and looked him right in the eye. As Larry chatted with Stevie and his other camper, Stevie suddenly hit Larry in the face! Larry was caught off guard. When he regained his composure, he realized that the hit was just Stevie's way of getting some space. Even Larry hadn't been prepared for that.

Stevie had been a drug baby at birth and a foster child since then. When Stevie was in a good mood, he was almost irresistibly loving and good-hearted. But when he was in a bad mood, he couldn't control his temper and had angry outbursts. The counselors and the other campers found it almost impossible to deal with him. But the Lord helped them to cope.

The third year that Stevie should have come to camp, he wasn't able to attend. He was such a well-known character that the camp counselors and returning campers made Stevie a present that year. They took a Royal Family Kids' Camps T-shirt and passed it around the camp for everyone to sign with best wishes. Then they sent it home to Stevie.

Stevie was a problem, but he was also a child of God. Everyone knew he would have been a terror if he had come to camp that year. But they also knew that it would break his heart to miss out on his favorite time all year—his week at camp. They sent him the T-shirt to tell him they missed him. Stevie's foster mother said he slept in that T-shirt every night for weeks. It meant so much to him to know that people remembered him and loved him.

Like Nehemiah building the wall, we're bound to come up against troubles, but also like Nehemiah, we're obligated to work through them. Nehemiah's troubles came in the form of two men, Sanballat and Tobiah, who didn't want the wall rebuilt. "When Sanballat heard that we were rebuilding the wall, he became angry and was greatly incensed," wrote Nehemiah. "He ridiculed the Jews, and in the presence of his associates and the army of Samaria, he said, 'What are those feeble Jews doing? Will they restore their wall? Will they offer sacrifices? Will they finish in a day? Can they bring the stones back to life from those heaps of rubble—burned as they are?'" (Neh. 4:1-2).

When we try to rebuild the lives of abused children, we shouldn't be surprised to hear the same kind of taunting arguments from our enemy, Satan: Do you expect to restore the lives of abused children who have been maimed at the most significant developmental years of their lives? Will you finish in a day? Can you bring these wrecked and bruised children back to life?

The taunts were meaningless to Nehemiah, and they are meaningless to us. We *can* rebuild the lives of broken children, but we must be committed to working through our problems.

As the American church responds to the needs of abused children, as we join together to rebuild these shattered lives, surely the prophecy of Isaiah is ours. "If you do away with the yoke of oppression, . . . and if you spend yourselves in behalf of the hungry and satisfy the needs of the oppressed, then your light will rise in the darkness, and your night will become like the noonday. . . . Your people will rebuild the ancient ruins and will raise up the age-old foundations; you will be called Repairer of Broken Walls, Restorer of Streets with Dwellings" (Isa. 58:9-12).

We can lift the yoke of oppression from little shoulders that never should have to carry it. We can satisfy the needs of the oppressed by giving abused children the wholesome love and affection that all children need. We will be the rebuilders, restorers, and repairers of young lives that otherwise have very little hope in this life. We will face many challenges to our work, but we can be ready to meet them.

When Nehemiah's enemies threatened him with military force, he simply instructed his workers to build the wall with one hand and carry their weapons with the other hand. What a beautiful model that is for us today. With one hand we can rebuild the lives of abused children, and with the other we can protect them from their enemies.

The Price of Abuse

The large words on the red, white, and blue sign by the side of the road captured my eye: The Price of Freedom Visibly Seen Here. Set behind the sign was the Veteran's Hospital of Batavia, New York. As Diane and I continued driving down the road, we could only imagine the price of freedom in the lives of the patients inside. Some were probably young, perhaps veterans of a recent war. Some had broken or missing limbs. Others would be older, reaping this small benefit of care in return for their earlier service.

But my mind, never far from the children I work with, couldn't let go of the sign's message. I thought of how often I see the visible price of child abuse, not on charts or in statistics, but in the children whose young bodies and tender souls bear the marks of the abusive war waged against them.

It's difficult to ignore the evidence of their experience. Some of it is as visible as the scars from deliberate burns or earlobes deformed from so much abuse. Some is not so obvious in children who look otherwise wholesome and healthy. But it *is* there—in the vacant, disconnected gaze or downcast eyes of a child too frightened to connect with humanity or reality. It is there—in the tempers that pepper the day with explosions of rage or in the nightmarish screams of restless children unable to give themselves over to the vulnerability of sleep. It is there—in the hearing impairments of some children whose eardrums have been broken and in the secret food-hoarding manners of others who can never be sure they'll have enough to fill their stomachs.

If I were to make a sign like the one we saw at the Veteran's Hospital, it would say, The Price of Child Abuse Visibly Seen Here. It is a message that can be depressing; each day we could update the sign with the ever-increasing count of children paying the price—from 1 million in 1985 to 3 million in 1993.

But when thoughts like that overwhelm me, I remember two things. The first is a statement by Mother Teresa: "I can't help them all, but I can help some." The second is the hope that God graciously and lovingly holds out to these children. It seems he almost had them in mind when he inspired David to write Psalm 40. "I waited patiently for the Lord; he turned to me and heard my cry. He lifted me out of the slimy pit, out of the mud and mire; he set my feet on a rock and gave me a firm place to stand. He put a new song in my mouth, a hymn of praise to our God. Many will see and fear and put their trust in the Lord" (Ps. 40:1-3).

The children *are* waiting for someone to bring God's love to them. The Scripture says that God turns to us and hears our cries, but for many abused children, their cries seem to be met only with violent acts of anger or appalling sexual or emotional abuse. God does hear them. But he also asks us, his church, to hear them and to turn to them. Will we lift up abused children from the slimy pit, out of the mud and mire? Will we reach into the closets where they are locked up and the lonely hiding places where they have withdrawn? We must, for we are God's hands extended to this dying world. As we follow his leading, he will set the feet of these children on a rock, give them a new song to sing, and validate their trust in him.

The price of child abuse and neglect *is* visibly seen, but not in a sign by the side of the road. It is seen in the scars of the children—until a friend like you reaches out to help.

Can We Make a Difference?

Can the church make a difference? Can I make a difference? Can you? Yes. Yes. Yes.

As you've read, the scars of child abuse are many and deep. Like the tender limbs of a tree, children can be bent only so far before they are broken. But *broken* isn't a frightening word to God; he once was broken for you and me. But he is whole and strong and powerful again today. The constant pain and betrayal of child abuse can press a little heart until it is crushed. But *crushed* isn't a frightening word to God; he was crushed beneath the weight of the transgressions of the world. But he defeated them.

"I will give you a new heart and put a new spirit in you," God says in Ezekiel 36:26. "I will remove from you your heart of stone and give you a heart of flesh." In self-defense, abused children may develop hearts of cold stone, but God can give them hearts of love. God is able to change forever the lives of these aching, needy children. But you and I must be willing to help. Working together, we *can* make a difference.

One of my favorite stories to illustrate the point happened along the southern coast of Australia, where thousands of starfish had washed up along the beach and were then drying out and dying in the sun. One frantic young boy raced about among them, picking up the starfish and heaving them back out to sea as quickly as he could. A jogger along the beach stopped and watched the boy in his work for a moment, then he said, "I understand what you're doing, but do you really think it will make a difference?"

The boy looked up at the man and then down at the dying starfish in his hand. "I don't know, mister," he said, "but I think it will make a difference for this one."

CHAPTER NINE

Stretcher-Bearing: Practical Steps for the Church to Help the Healing

IF you are familiar with the New Testament, you know the story of the four friends who dismantled the roof of a house to get their sick friend to Jesus. "Soon the house where he was staying was so packed with visitors that there wasn't room for a single person more, not even outside the door. And he preached the Word to them. Four men arrived carrying a paralyzed man on a stretcher. They couldn't get to Jesus through the crowd, so they dug through the clay roof above his head and lowered the sick man on his stretcher, right down in front of Jesus" (Mark 2:2-4, TLB). Jesus honored the eagerness of the paralyzed man's friends; he forgave the man's sins and healed him. But what would have become of him if the four friends had not been willing to work so hard to get him into the Master's presence?

Today millions of children are broken, bruised, and emotionally paralyzed because of child abuse. They need strong friends like you to work hard to get them into the Master's presence so that he can heal them. The church's response must be that of stretcher-bearers. We must take the children to Jesus.

When we sat down to write this book, the parts about the children—their stories and their words—wrote themselves. But when it came to writing about prevention of child abuse and treatment for offenders, the writing became more difficult. We sense a number of natural barriers.

The obvious one is this: The children we deal with through the camps are generally those whose parents or primary caregivers have been proven so abusive or neglectful that the children have been removed from the home. But hundreds of thousands of children are never removed from abusive environments. And the goal of the foster-care system is—and ought to be—the eventual return of the children to their homes.

While it's easy for us to teach children to protect themselves from strangers, we can't protect them from everybody; in 90 percent of physical-abuse cases the perpetrator isn't a stranger. The abuser is a caregiver or a close friend of the family.[1] How can children protect themselves from an abuser who is their parent, caregiver, or guardian?

Children cannot.

Prevention efforts must focus on the abuser, who must be willing to receive help and who probably isn't the kind of person to read a book like this. The problem of how to reach the abuser seems overwhelming.

The other barrier that can bar the efforts of the church to respond to the problem of child abuse is that we Christians tend to regard hurting a child as the most offensive of crimes.

We may find ourselves too angry to pray for the child abuser and too resistant to work toward his or her reclamation. This is a natural, human response. But it *cannot* be the response of the church on such a critical issue.

We need to accept the example of Jesus, who extended his loving-kindness to the vilest offender, yet at the same time he loved children with all of his perfect nature. A willingness to forgive and help child abusers *does not* erode our compassion for the children. If we can be Christlike enough to overcome our reluctance to deal charitably with child abusers, we will find the opportunity to help them and to save children from further abuse.

One thing to remember about parents who physically abuse their children is that they don't generally do so out of malice or sadism. Rather, they abuse in times of frustration and crisis. They usually are from violent homes themselves and have had no formal training in parenting skills. The only way they know to respond to the pressures of raising children is the same way their parents responded to them. They don't *want* to hurt their children, and they don't derive any pleasure from it. But they haven't figured out what else to do.

Perhaps we as Christians can understand and forgive child abusers if we know some of the causes of child abuse and neglect. Psychologists have discovered various types of people who abuse children and the thinking patterns that motivate them to do so.

Causes for Abuse
Abusive parents create child abusers
Between 85 percent and 90 percent of today's abusive parents were abused when they were children. This is not to say that

all people who were abused as children will abuse their children. However, if parents feel tempted to respond to life's pressure by abusing their children or by thinking about abusing them, they should do the following:

1. Parents should find the phone number and location of the nearest crisis nursery. The next time they think they may abuse their children, they should take them to the crisis nursery instead. Children's workers there will take care of the children until the parents are more able to cope.

2. If the community does not have a crisis nursery, parents should ask a trusted friend or family member to be willing to take their children when they are in crisis. When parents feel stressed, they should give themselves a "time-out" from their children. They can take a walk or count to 100 or listen to some music, but they don't need to hurt their children.

3. Parents who are tempted to abuse their children can go to their pastor or community information-and-referral service and find out where to secure the help they need to overcome these tendencies. Whatever they do, *they must get help!* They don't need to perpetuate abuse by abusing their children.

Stress leads to abuse

An abusive parent will lash out at a child during times of crisis, even if the crisis is not necessarily related to the child's actions or behavior.[2] A job or unemployment, money worries, and family tensions can be too much for the child abuser who has never learned how to cope with stress. Part of this stress may also involve the difficulty of trying to raise children alone. Too often one of the spouses is absent or uninvolved, and the abusive parent may feel totally responsible for the child.

Drug and alcohol abuse seem to play a major role in child abuse as well. In 40 percent or more of reported cases of child abuse and neglect, drugs or alcohol are also involved.[3]

High-risk children are often abused

Studies show that certain children are in a high-risk group for child abuse.[4] Children who suffer from a birth defect, a chronic illness, a resemblance to someone disliked by the parents, or some other distinctive mark may be in the high-risk group. Younger children are in a higher-risk group because they are easiest to abuse and least likely to respond to reason, which can lead an abusive parent to use force. Children who were born prematurely or were the result of very difficult births are also in high-risk groups for abuse, possibly because the mother blames the baby for the pain surrounding the birth.

In such cases inexperienced and unprepared parents may find it difficult to cope with the child's problems or the anger they feel toward the child. They may even develop the misperception that the child is responsible for the problems and anger, that the child is somehow "evil."[5]

Unrealistic demands for love lead to abuse

In some cases parents who feel rejected and forgotten by their own families may expect their children to provide the love they feel is lacking.[6] This, of course, is an unrealistic expectation placed on an infant or child. It is the parent who must provide love and affection at these stages of a young life. When this parental role is thrust on young children, they cannot possibly comply. But the result of this failure may be abuse.

Unrealistic expectations of child development lead to abuse
Parents who have no knowledge of child development or who have not been equipped with proper parenting skills may have unrealistic expectations of what their children should be able to do.[7] For instance, an uneducated or inexperienced mother who is trying to cope on her own may be particularly eager for her infant to become toilet trained and stop making messes. As a result, she may try to toilet train her child when he or she is only a year old. Few children are ready for toilet training at that age, and for many children, this training goes on past the age of three. But an inexperienced mother may not realize that her child is incapable of the skill she requires of him or her. She may mistakenly believe the child continues to dirty diapers merely to spite her. Abuse may result.

Excessive punishment leads to abuse
Punishing children beyond what their minor misbehavior calls for sometimes crosses the line into child abuse. When an abusive parent is under stress and a child misbehaves, the parent may actually find physical and emotional release through vigorously punishing the child. In this situation, standard child misbehavior becomes the path to abuse. For the inexperienced parent wondering how to distinguish an appropriate punishment from excessive punishment, Angela Carl's book *Child Abuse! What You Can Do about It* offers these helpful guidelines:

1. Is the purpose of the punishment to train the child or to express your anger?

2. Would a less severe punishment be equally as effective?[8]

Misplaced anger leads to abuse

For some abusive parents, the child has actually become an abuse surrogate for someone or something the parent would like to hurt and punish.[9] This can be seen in the case of a stepparent who sees in the child a constant reminder that the spouse once had other relationships and attachments. In this case a sort of jealousy drives the stepparent to abuse the child. In other cases the child may be resented for reminding the mother or father of the spouse who may have abandoned the family and caused great pain. The need for retribution toward the absent spouse translates into abuse of the child. Parents who suffer with poor self-respect may see and punish *themselves* in their children. If parents dislike themselves, it is difficult for them to respect or love their children.

Although the crimes abusive parents commit against children are abhorrent, it's easy to see that many of the causes underlying the actions of abusers are pitiable: low self-image, pain at the hands of parents or others, ignorance of child development, and overreaction to stress. In spite of what we may think of abusive parents, their problems are human. They need our prayers, and they need our help.

Because most abuse of children is perpetrated by caregivers and parents, we must focus our efforts for *prevention* on helping abusers quit abusing. Since adults who were abused as children are the ones with the highest potential to abuse their own children, we can help stop the cycle that is handed down from generation to generation if we can help *this* generation of child abusers to quit.

There *is* hope that we can put an end to child abuse. One of the first and most basic steps that you and your church can take in preventing child abuse is to know the indicators of child abuse and to whom they can be reported.

Signs and Signals of Child Abuse

How do you know if a child you know is being abused? Beware of several physical indicators:

- severe bruises, human bite marks, and welts on the face, torso, back, backside, or legs
- various types of severe burns, including cigarette or cigar burns, rope burns, and any burn that leaves a clearly defined mark of the sort of instrument used to cause the burn
- bone breaks or fractures; in particular, fractured skull, nose, or facial structure or the presence of more than one fracture or fractures in the healing stages
- constant vomiting or swollen or tender limbs or abdomen
- lacerations or abrasions of mouth, eyes, genitalia, back, legs, or torso[10]

Children who routinely exhibit symptoms such as these may be victims of child abuse. Even if these wounds appear to be healing, ask the children how the wounds happened. If the children have no explanation or an unrealistic explanation or if they say that an adult hurt them, child abuse must be suspected.

Although they are not as easy to define as are the physical indicators, here are some behavioral indicators:

- in general, an irrational fear of their parents or of going home
- extremes in behavior
- fear of adults[11]

Neglect may be the most common form of child abuse. Parents or caregivers neglect their children when they do not provide them with the minimum standard of care: food, clothing, shelter, hygiene, and education.[12] If neglect is the result of financial hardship, the family can usually find assistance in the form of government or private aid.

How do you know if children are being neglected? Children may appear at school or church in tattered clothes or looking dirty and unkempt at one time or another. *That* doesn't indicate neglect; it may merely indicate busy parents. Some signs of neglect may include the following:

- children chronically appear tattered, dirty, and unkempt
- children are hungry all the time
- children frequently miss school
- children appear in obvious need of medical care[13]

In order for you and the members of your church to begin the process of prevention, you must know which state or government office to call to report suspected child abuse and neglect. The correct authorities to which child abuse must be reported vary from state to state. Generally these authorities have names such as Child Protective Services, Health and Human Services, and Social Services. Child abuse and neglect also can be reported directly to the police department.

As a service to your church, find out the office and phone number for your state. Provide the members of your church with the list of child-abuse indicators and the phone number for reporting suspected abuse. Remember that in most states it is *mandatory* to report child abuse whenever you have reasonable grounds to suspect it is happening; failure to report is a violation of the law. Churches that suspect child abuse are also required to report it; failure to do so can result in liability if the abuse is later reported. Please do not let a child suffer or be permanently damaged because you are embarrassed or afraid to report what you suspect!

The System

Although the exact procedure varies from state to state, here is a general outline of what happens when a case of suspected child abuse is reported:

1. Your state's child-protective services agency or the local police conduct a case investigation to determine whether there is evidence of abuse or neglect.
2. If the investigation concludes that child abuse is present in the home, the authorities determine whether the risk of abuse or neglect is great enough to remove the child from the home. If the risk is not great, the child will remain in the home. Agency workers will suggest counseling for parents and conduct follow-up visits at later dates to insure that the abuse or neglect has ceased.

3. If the investigation concludes that the risk is high enough to remove the child from the home, the agency will generally have to show this in a juvenile court hearing, at which a judge may order the child's removal from the home. If the abuse is severe, the agency may also initiate criminal proceedings against the abusive adult.

4. If the juvenile court judge does not agree that there is enough risk of child abuse to warrant the child's removal from the home, the child remains in the home with scheduled follow-up and protection to be insured by the child-protective services agency. If the child is removed from the home, he or she is placed in the foster-care system, and if no criminal charges are pending against the caretaker or parent, he or she is usually given a recovery program to follow before the child will be allowed to return to the home.[14]

5. If the parent makes no effort to follow the program, the child may be placed permanently in foster care or be made available for adoption. If the parent completes the program and proves to the agency and the court that there is now little risk of repeated abuse, the child can be returned to the home.

Although this is only a general outline, it is an example of how the state uses intervention in the prevention of child abuse. As with all things human, the system does not always work to the best interest of the child, but it is an important way to protect children from abuse and neglect in the home. Appendix B lists the phone numbers and addresses of organizational and support-group resources.

What You Can Do Now

You and your church can become involved in several other methods of prevention to help abused children now.

- Phone hot lines provide help for abused children and abusive parents twenty-four hours a day. Members of your church can obtain training to answer the phone hot line, which parents call when they feel overwhelming stress and may abuse their children. The phone counselor provides parents with reassurance, help, suggestions, and the name and address of the nearest crisis nursery.

- Crisis nurseries can also prevent child abuse by providing a place where a parent can leave the endangered child in times of crisis. In some cases the nursery is essentially a shelter and an extension of state child-protective services. The facility is set up to house children who have been removed from their homes until they can be returned or placed in foster care. But this doesn't have to be the case. Your church can support or sponsor a crisis nursery that accepts children from parents twenty-four hours a day, no questions asked.

In the case of both the crisis nursery and the phone hot line, good publicity is key. Parents must *know* not only that these services exist but also how to get them. Advertising, flyers, bumper stickers, and public-service announcements on local radio and television all can be useful tools in getting out the message that there *is* help for the child abuser.

The church in America can also make an astounding impact in this area by recruiting Christian foster families. If every church in America recruited just one foster family, every child now awaiting placement in the foster-care system could be placed tomorrow in a Christian home.[15] Becoming a state-licensed foster parent is neither expensive nor complicated. Foster parenting is not limited to married couples but can include single people, senior citizens, and childless couples. Almost anyone who loves children and wants to help can become a foster parent. Even couples and single people who have full-time jobs can become foster parents, providing day care for young foster children or taking only foster children who are already in school.

Typically the state not only trains prospective foster parents but also screens them for prior arrest records and screens the home for safety features. Once foster parents have been licensed, they generally will be required to continue with training, which in some states is as little as six hours per *year.* Once a foster child is placed in the foster home, the state will reimburse the parents for expenses of that child, provide the child's medical care, provide any psychiatric care, and meet any other special needs. But potential foster parents need not fear that the state will give them a foster child who is so severely in need of therapy or medical help that they can't handle the child. Foster parents can specify the various characteristics of the children with whom they would like to work. Foster parents can request children of a certain age range, race, sex, and level of emotional or physical disability.

The state continues to provide support for foster parents. The child's caseworker is available to help foster parents twenty-four hours a day, providing a window to all the help the state provides. Many communities provide support groups for foster parents. If at any point the foster parents can no longer handle the child, they can call the caseworker and have the child returned to state custody.

In most states, loving foster parents are in such great demand that they can "write their own ticket" for children they will have in their home. Foster parents can specify how long they are willing to keep a child. For instance, some people take in foster children every summer or only during the school year. Other people take in foster children every other year. Still others take in children all year long.

People who already have their own children may worry that the presence of foster children will somehow corrupt their children. But it may be more likely that the children of Christian parents actually become *better* Christians after foster children have been in their home. This allows the biological children the wonderful opportunity to observe their parents in a *living example* of the compassion of Christ, pouring out their love on a needy child.

If you are saying to yourself, *If I had a foster child, I would love that child too much to give him or her back,* please don't let that stop you from becoming a foster parent. Yes, it will hurt to let the child go, but compare that pain with the alternatives for that child: He or she will either go into an institution or remain in an abusive situation. Remember that any child placed in the foster-care system has been the victim of incomprehensible pain.

Will your pain at losing a child be anything in comparison to that? Either we will suffer a little for the children, or they will suffer a lot, alone. If you're a Christian, remember that Jesus—who was not afraid to suffer for you—has commanded you to love these lost children, even when it hurts. If you possibly can, open your home to a foster child. And by all means, recruit foster families in your church.

Prevention = Treatment

Because the earliest research showed that abused children grow up to abuse their children, treatment of both abusers and the abused was among the very first methods of child-abuse prevention. Treatment of parents focuses on helping them to overcome abusive tendencies and work through frustrations in nonharmful ways. Treatment of abused children focuses on repairing psychological and physical damage as well as keeping abused children from becoming abusive parents. Treatment may specifically target parents, children, or the entire family unit.

In their excellent book *Child Abuse and the Church: A New Mission,* James Mead and Glenn Balch, Jr., describe various treatment programs that the church can sponsor or support.

1. *Individual treatment.* Individual counseling with a qualified therapist may benefit some child abusers. Such programs can be sponsored by community or church groups and may already be available in your area. Church support of this treatment is vitally needed.

2. *Rent-a-Grandparent program.* This program allows retired people who have already raised their children to give their years of experience and knowledge to families that may be struggling with child abuse. Grandparents attend training sessions to learn the best way to help. They then spend an average of one day a week with the needy family, advising and reas-

suring both parents and children.

The value of the grandparent figure cannot be overstated. While children receive discipline and instruction from parents, they receive nothing but love from grandparents. At our camps an older volunteer couple is always designated as camp Grandma and Grandpa, and the effect on the children is healing. Many of them do not have or do not often get to see their natural grandparents, but the unconditional love of these surrogates is ravenously consumed.

If you are an older person with love to give to children, invest your time in the Rent-a-Grandparent program. Not only will you help and give comfort to the parent, but you also will bring new life to a child. If no Rent-a-Grandparent organization exists in your area, organize the older people in your church to start one.

3. *Volunteers in child-abuse prevention.* It is highly likely that your state's child-protective services agency has a program to train volunteers to help families identified as abusive or neglectful. As a volunteer, you would visit the home of the family you are assigned to, help the parent overcome abusive behavior, and help insure proper conditions for the child. You might also be on call for that family in times of stress and crisis. Contact your area's child-protective services agency for more information, and organize adult volunteers in your church to get involved.

Group treatment not only helps abusive parents overcome these tendencies but also aids in the healing of emotional scars for abused children. We have found that wherever we go, child-abuse survivors are simply relieved to be able to talk about what happened to them. For too long, child abuse has literally been a secret world.

4. *Incest-survivor groups.* Victims of incest are finding help and relief through group therapy, admitting what happened to them, sharing their feelings with other survivors, and going on to overcome the problem. It's important that groups like these keep their eyes on the prize: living an emotionally healthy life in spite of the past, rather than focusing on the horrors of the past. With proper direction these groups can provide life-changing experiences for the members.[16]

Other treatment that focuses on the abused child must take several factors into consideration. The psychological issues include lack of trust and self-esteem, depression, and anxiety.[17] Treatment for the abused child includes individual and group therapy and should be designed to address the following issues:

- self-respect
- trust
- anxiety
- interpersonal skills
- expression of feelings
- fun

However, treatment for the abused child must address not only psychological issues but also developmental issues. It has been estimated that up to 90 percent of abused children suffer developmental delays—that is, they may lag behind other children of their age in such areas as speech, motor skills, emotional development, perceptual abilities, and social skills.[18]

In this area it is sometimes up to public schools, teachers, school nurses, and administrators to spot the signals or results of child abuse and respond appropriately. That means it is terribly important for school workers to understand the symptoms of child abuse and be able to recognize them. Yet very few colleges that train today's educators are preparing students for this skill. One way that you and the members of your church can help is by offering training for school workers so that they can know and recognize the symptoms of child abuse. If you are an educator yourself, you can work to see that your fellow teachers or administrators are properly trained in this area.

But once child abuse has been recognized, reported, and prevented, the abused child may still suffer developmental delay and will require specialized help in school. This issue also deserves the attention of professional educators. While many of these children will fall into the realm of those in need of special education, they are also different from special education children who have not been abused. Abused children may need a different course of study to help them regain ground lost to abuse.

Get the Word Out

The other valuable area of child-abuse prevention is education, which is vital in breaking the cycle of child abuse. If you could have met Carrie, a young girl who came to camp last year, you'd know why. Carrie was eight years old, and she was intrigued when she met Cindi, the wife of one of the camp counselors. Cindi was in the eighth month of pregnancy, and Carrie was curious.

"Are you going to have a baby?" she asked.

"Yes," Cindi said. "In just about a month."

"May I touch your baby?" Carrie asked next, reaching out to stroke Cindi's protruding tummy. She smiled at Cindi and her soon-to-be-born baby, but in just a few seconds her young face became stern. Carrie shook her finger at Cindi as she said, "If you have a little girl, don't ever scold her or beat her or make her sit in the corner for a long, long time. You just love her and cuddle her, OK?"

Carrie's mother may never have cuddled her. It's evident that her mother probably beat her and scolded her. Statistically Carrie is in the high-risk group of potential child abusers when she grows up. But in real life, somebody stepped in and showed Carrie that there are better ways to raise children, that young girls were made to be loved and cuddled, not beaten. Education *can* help to prevent child abuse.

Because we know that child abuse happens when parents aren't prepared to cope with children, it is essential that we do everything possible to provide tomorrow's parents with the skills they will need to be moms and dads. High school is not too early to begin teaching young men and women parenting skills. Because many young women give birth before high-school graduation, parenting education at the junior high level may be more appropriate. Schools should require parenting courses; churches can offer free parenting classes. Not the tiniest bit of preparation that we can instill will be in vain if it saves the life of just one child.

Expectant mothers in particular must be trained in parenting. Many hospitals today offer parenting classes along with childbirth classes. Doctors are referring their pregnant patients to parenting classes, and pediatricians are sending young parents to class. If your church chooses to offer parenting classes, make sure local doctors and hospitals are aware of the service so they can refer expectant moms to you.

Just Do It

The American church can respond in so many ways to the crisis of child abuse. Your local church can lead the way. You don't have to take children into your home; you don't have to become a psychologist and try to counsel abusive parents. You just have to love children, pray for them, and be open to God's call to help them. God will do the rest.

For the past four years our friends Walt and Loretta Smith have worked as counselors at one of the summer camps, where one precious girl became attached to them. Peggy was waiting for a family to adopt her, and she wanted that family to be Walt and Loretta. However, since Walt and Loretta are already grandparents of eight children, they could not adopt Peggy. The young girl understood this, but she said she wished she could at least change her last name to Smith so she could share their last name and pretend she was their daughter.

In a nearby city, a couple named Smith were on the waiting list to adopt a young girl. When the big day came, they selected Peggy. She received her wish: Her last name became Smith. Peggy received the answer to her prayers! God will go to great lengths for these children. He asks us only to be willing to help.

When church families face the crisis of child sexual abuse,
their pastor may be the one they turn to for help. The following information from Christian counselor and pastor Dr.
Richard Dobbins, director of EMERGE Ministries, Inc.,
assists pastors trying to help sexual-abuse victims and their
families move through recovery.[1]

As a pastor, your role in dealing with child sexual-abuse victims and their families should not be to accept full responsibility for treatment but rather to see that they are placed in
counseling with competent Christian mental-health professionals. However, you can have a major impact in immediate
counseling. When you learn of an incident of child sexual
abuse, pray with the hurting family, help them through the
legal and medical aspects, and maintain close pastoral follow-
up.

Keep in mind several treatment goals for the child and family:

- Support, protect, and counsel the child.
- Help the parents protect their child and deal with
  their own emotional pain.
- In the case of incest, help the nonabusing parent to

separate the child from the abusing parent. Support the nonabusing parent.

- If the abuser is a member of your church, confront him or her with the sin and illness of child sexual abuse and make sure he or she gets effective counseling. Child sexual abuse must be recognized for what it is: a sin against God and children and a compulsive illness that victimizes children.

Immediate Crisis

By law you are required to report child sexual abuse to the local child-protection agency and/or police. Know the reporting laws of your state as well as the appropriate professionals and community agencies that provide help and counsel in sexual-abuse crises. In the case of incest, depending on how the family is dealing with the situation, you may decide to report the case without their knowledge. However, because the report may result in the temporary placement of the child with a foster family, it is better if the family can be made aware of the report. That way, they can be involved in placing the child with a trustworthy grandparent or another close relative.

When you are called on to help families through the crisis of child sexual abuse, you will probably find the parents' reaction to be outrage, anger, and panic. Both the parents and the child probably will be in crisis when they come to you. People in acute crisis must be seen within twenty-four hours—sooner if possible—by the critical members of the "support team": you as pastor, medical personnel, and law-enforcement or child-protective services. Have prayer with the victim and parent or parents immediately, and schedule a home visit as soon as possible. If you are not available when the crisis arises, have a trained church staff member make contact with the family.

Within Twenty-Four Hours of Sexual Abuse

If you and the parents learn of the molestation within eighteen to twenty-four hours of the act, pray with them and help them follow this procedure:

1. Take the child to a medical center for a physical examination, whether or not there is an apparent injury. Accompany the family for support.
2. Do not wash the child or put clean clothes on him or her. The abuser's body fluids, which may be found on the child or clothing, will provide evidence in the event of criminal prosecution.
3. The parent should discreetly inform the person in charge at the medical facility what has happened and ask for gentle care of the child. Stand with the parent in this difficult task.
4. Inform the police, who will work together with the medical center staff to gather evidence for prosecution. Ask for only one police representative to question the child, preferably an officer of the same sex as the child.
5. Compile a list of names and telephone numbers of all persons involved in the case: medical personnel, police, etc. This may be helpful for future reference.

As soon after the molestation as possible, help the parents to convey specific messages to the child:

- *"It's OK to tell me about this."* If the abuser is a family member or friend, do not exhibit anger toward the person or talk about what will happen to him or her (jail term, etc.). The child may feel guilty for "telling on" the abuser (particularly if there was no physical pain involved in the act). Parents can allay that guilt by making it clear that it's OK for the child to tell.
- *"I believe you."* Children rarely lie about something so intimate and so personal, and even preschoolers can report incidents of sexual abuse with enough accuracy and clarity to make listeners understand what has happened. Parents should not give the impression that they don't believe the child.
- *"It's OK to feel angry."* A crime has been committed against the child, so normal child-to-adult emotions of kindness, trust, and obedience are replaced by anger and hurt. Parents must assure the child that anger and pain are reasonable and normal in this situation.
- *"This is not your fault."* Help the parents assure the child that this is not something the child *did,* but rather it is something *done to* the child.
- *"I love you and care about you."* The child must be reassured of parental love. Parents should express how sorry they are that this has happened.

Dealing with the Abuser

Your purpose in confronting abusers with their sin and illness is threefold: to help them realize their addiction, to help them to control and conquer the addiction, and to guide them to seek and receive forgiveness.

An abuser from outside the family

If the abuser is not a family member, the situation is somewhat easier to manage from a pastoral counseling point of view. Naturally, the abuse must be reported to the authorities immediately. Meet with the parents to let them vent their feelings and organize a plan for dealing with the crisis. Then meet with the child, and allow him or her to express feelings also. Assure the child that there is no reason to feel guilty or afraid. Remind the child that he or she will be protected. Then refer the family to a competent Christian mental-health professional or agency. You should, of course, continue appropriate pastoral follow-up with the parents and the child.

An abuser from within the church family

If the *abuser* also attends your church, you must meet with him or her to help the abuser deal with his or her guilt and need for therapy. Alert the abuser to the legal complications he or she may face, since the abuse must be reported. You may help the abuser find an attorney if that is necessary. Protect other children in your church by suspending any leadership roles that may have put the abuser in close or unattended contact with children. Finally, refer the abuser to a competent Christian mental-health agency or professional, and maintain appropriate pastoral follow-up. (For information about protecting your church from charges of abuse by volunteers/staff, write or call for the booklet *How to Protect the Children and Keep the Church Out of Court*. EMERGE Ministries, Inc., 900 Mull Avenue, Akron, Ohio 44313 or phone (216) 867-5603.)

An abuser from within the family

The most difficult circumstance is learning that an abuser is from inside the family unit. In most incest cases, the victim is a daughter and the abuser is the victim's father or stepfather or the male friend of the mother. However, it is possible for incest to involve boys as well as girls, fathers as well as mothers. It was recently reported that in three of four cases in which boys were abused by men, the men were involved in a relationship with a female relative of the boy. To avoid confusion, the advice given in the following paragraphs will refer to the abusing parent and the nonabusing parent.

If victims of sexual abuse are going to tell the nonabusing parent about the molestation rather than keep the secret, they will usually do so within twenty-four hours of the event. In too many cases, the nonabusing parent is unwilling to support the child, telling the child, "Don't talk like that about your father (mother)." The nonabusing parent may promise to make the abuser stop, but without treatment that won't happen. The parent is *more likely* to seek help if the abuser is the child's stepparent or sibling and not the child's natural parent. In any case, the abuse must be reported to the proper authorities.

If the abuser is the child's natural parent, the nonabusing parent is forced to choose between supporting the child or his or her spouse. If the nonabusing parent chooses to support the child, a marital crisis arises. The nonabusing parent must reconcile with, separate from, or divorce the abuser. If the nonabusing parent is reluctant to come to the child's aid, you, as the pastor, will be placed in the middle of the conflict. You must report the abuse and help the nonabusing parent find the courage to break out of denial and get help for the child, the spouse, and the rest of the family. Help the nonabusing spouse face the following questions:

- Is the abuser more important to me than my child?
- Should I seek counseling for myself and my child?
- Should I bar the abuser from seeing the children until he (she) gets help?
- Should I seek a divorce or separation and therapy?

Avoiding divorce in such a situation is possible only with extended spiritual, legal, and psychiatric help. The abuser must accept the fact that he or she may never again be allowed to be alone with small children.

If the Child Tells You First

If the child tells you, the pastor, about sexual abuse by a family member before he or she has told anyone else, you must help the child find the courage to tell the nonabusing parent. You are also required to report the abuse to the proper authorities. You will have to confront the child with the questions he or she is no doubt asking inside:

- *"Will I betray one of my parents if I tell the other?"* Fear or blind loyalty may be behind the child's reluctance to tell, but you must help the child realize that sharing the secret will help both parents.
- *"What will my mother (father) think?"* You cannot deny that the nonabusing parent will be shocked, but help the child see that the nonabusing parent will overcome that shock and come to his or her aid. The nonabusing parent's love will do what's best for the child.
- *"What will my father (mother) think if I tell?"* The abusing parent has undoubtedly flattered, threatened, and/or intimidated the child to keep him or her from

telling "their secret." Let the child know that protection from the abusing parent will come only if he or she shares the secret.

- *"What will happen to my family?"* The child does not want to be responsible for the family's possible breakup. Your job as pastor is to help the child see that *the abuser,* and not the victim, is responsible for what happens to the family. Help the child see that the family's chances for survival and restoration to health are better only if he or she *does* tell.

- *"What happens if I don't tell?"* If the child has other, especially younger, siblings, let the child know that they are at risk too. If the child is not willing to tell, he or she will be forced to continue being abused because abusers have little or no awareness of wrongdoing. Their consciences have been seared, so they are not likely to stop molesting on their own. If the child wants to protect himself or herself from further abuse and protect siblings as well, the child must tell.

Reintegrating the Family after Incest

Every responsible professional person reports and seeks treatment for known cases of child abuse or sexual abuse, and the case of incest is no different. When as the pastor you have counseled through the crisis moments with the child and family, refer them to an appropriate Christian mental-health professional or agency. Adequate treatment of intrafamilial child sexual abuse involves the whole family. Initially each of the involved persons—the victim, the nonabusing parent, and the abusing parent—needs individual treatment. Eventually the entire family is counseled together.

If the marriage does not end in divorce and treatment is successful, there are important pastoral considerations for reintegration of families after incest. Reassure the child that he or she is not responsible or being blamed for the sexual abuse. Help create clear lines of communication and instill trust between the nonabusing parent and child. Make sure the child feels protected from the abusing parent. Remind the child, the nonabusing parent, and the abusing parent that the secret has been exposed and that there will be no more secrets.

Jesus—The Child Advocate

If you have not yet faced the crisis of child sexual abuse in your church, you very well may. Many researchers estimate that the actual number of sexual abuse cases that occur in America is 3 million a year—by far the vast majority go unreported. This figure means between 5 percent and 15 percent of our nation's children are being sexually abused. The crisis is real, and it could confront you as a pastor.

Be ready for the task of helping a child impacted by child sexual abuse, even if you have not yet been confronted with it. Explore options of Christian mental-health care in your area so you can immediately recommend further counseling. Find out your state's laws about reporting sexual abuse. Train your staff to deal with this kind of crisis if you are unavailable.

In cases of child sexual abuse and especially incest, you must be squarely on the *child's* side. Although the nonabusing parent will be in crisis, it is the little one who has been victimized and who does not have the tools to cope with it. You must be the child's advocate. You must protect, support, and counsel the child first. In the case of incest, your next duty is to enlist the support of the nonabusing parent in protecting the child and help the nonabusing parent find treatment. Your final responsibility is to see that the abuser gets treatment so the cycle is not repeated.

Christian ministers should be the greatest child advocates of all, for we follow in the footsteps of our Lord and Savior, whose heart for children is clear in this New Testament passage:

> At that time the disciples came to Jesus, saying, "Who then is greatest in the kingdom of heaven?"
>
> Then Jesus called a little child to Him, set him in the midst of them, and said, "Assuredly, I say to you, unless you are converted and become as little children, you will by no means enter the kingdom of heaven. . . . Whoever receives one little child like this in My name receives Me. Whoever causes one of these little ones who believe in Me to sin, it would be better for him if a millstone were hung around his neck, and he were drowned in the depth of the sea." (Matt. 18:1-6, NKJV)

The little ones are dear to the heart of God. You will need prayer, understanding, counseling, compassion, and love to restore a child victim of sexual abuse. But because Jesus has a special love for the children, he will help you in this important task.

These organizations may provide you and your church family
with additional support as you minister to child-abuse victims.

American Humane Association—Children's Division, American Association for Protecting Children, 9725 W. Hamp-
ton, Denver, CO 80231; phone: (303) 695-0811
Canadian Society for the Prevention of Cruelty to Children,
356 First St., Box 700, Midland, ON L4R 9Z9 Canada
Child Welfare League of America, 1346 Connecticut Ave.
NW, Washington, D.C. 20036; phone: (202) 638-2952
Childhelp National Child Abuse Hotline: (800) 422-4453
[or (800) 4-A-CHILD] P.O. Box 630, Hollywood, CA
90028
For Kid's Sake, Inc., P.O. Box 313, Lake Elsinore, CA 92331-
0313; phone: (714) 244-9001
Heart to Heart, Inc., 2115 S.E. Adams, Milwaukie, OR
97222-7773; phone: (503) 654-3870
Henry Kempe National Center for Child Abuse, 1205
Oneida St., Denver, CO 80220; phone: (303) 321-3963
National Center for Missing and Exploited Children, 2101
Wilson Blvd., Arlington, VA 22201; phone: (703) 235-
3900, (800) 843-5678
National Center on Child Abuse and Neglect, U.S. Dept. of

Health and Human Services, P.O. Box 1182, Washington, DC 20013; phone: (703) 385-7565

National Committee for Prevention of Child Abuse and Neglect, 332 S. Michigan Ave., Suite 1250, Chicago, IL 60604-4357; phone: (312) 663-3520

National Resource Center on Child Sexual Abuse, 107 Lincoln St., Huntsville, AL 35801; phone: (800) 543-7006 [or (800) KIDS 006]

Parents United, Inc.; Daughters & Sons United; Adults Molested as Children United, P.O. Box 952, San Jose, CA 95108; phone: (408) 453-7616

Royal Family Kids' Camps, Inc., 1068 Salinas Ave., Costa Mesa, CA 92626; phone: (714) 556-1420

The Spiritual Dimension in Victim Services, P.O. Box 6736, Denver, CO 80206; phone: (303) 740-8171

Workshops and consulting services are available to assist local
churches to implement a prevention plan. The ones presented
below are taken from Richard R. Hammar, Steven W.
Klipowicz, and James F. Cobble, Jr. *Reducing the Risk of Child
Sexual Abuse in Your Church: A Complete and Practical Guidebook for Prevention and Risk Reduction* (Matthews, N.C.:
Christian Ministry Resources, 1993). Workshops can include
up to five participating congregations. Special arrangements
can be made for denominationally sponsored events. Prices
vary depending on the number of participating churches. All
workshops and consulting services are conducted by Church
Law & Tax Report staff. For more information call Christian
Ministry Resources at (704) 841-8066.

☐ *Workshop 1—Launching a Prevention Program.* This workshop helps church leaders understand the importance of a
  prevention program and provides detailed guidance on
  launching a program in a local church. A typical format
  would include sessions on Friday night and Saturday.
☐ *Workshop 2—Training Church Workers.* This workshop provides training to church workers to reduce the risk of child
  or sexual abuse within the church. Attention is given to un-

derstanding the nature of abuse and procedures designed
to protect both children and workers.

☐ *Consulting Service—Launching a Prevention Program.* The
consulting service includes the Sexual Abuse Prevention
Resource Kit plus one hour of telephone consulting in
launching a program in your local church. Price: $125

Sexual Abuse Prevention Resource Kit

This resource kit includes a training video and leader's
guide, an audiocassette tape, and a resource book. The regular
price for these resources is $58.85, but the kit fee is only
$49.95. If desired, each resource can be ordered separately
(the individual price is listed following each description).

☐ *Sexual Abuse Prevention Resource Kit.* Includes all of the following resources. Price: $49.95

☐ *Training Video and Leader's Guide.* The first segment of the
video helps church leaders and members understand why
churches must take action to reduce the risk of sexual
abuse. Segment 2 covers policies regarding sexual abuse
and the church. The tape comes with a leader's guide that
provides detailed instructions on how to use the tape for
training purposes. The tape and leader's guide provide
important support in implementing a prevention program
in the local church. Price: $39.95

☐ *What Church Leaders Should Know about Sexual Abuse and
the Church*—audiocassette. This tape helps church leaders
understand how the problem of sexual abuse affects local
churches and provides a powerful motivation to launch a
prevention program. Price: $9.95

☐ *Reducing the Risk of Sexual Abuse in Your Church*—resource book. Composed of three parts, this book provides detailed guidance on how to enlist the support of key leaders, formulate policies and procedures, and train workers. Price: $8.95

All prices are subject to change.

To order, write Christian Ministry Resources, P.O. Box 2301, Matthews, NC 28106, or call (800) 222-1840.

CHAPTER 1

1. Names of most adults and all children in this book have been changed to preserve confidentiality.
2. Fact sheet for the movie *Scared Silent: Exposing and Ending Child Abuse,* hosted by Oprah Winfrey and Arnold Shapiro Productions.
3. Angela Carl, *Child Abuse* (Cincinnati: Standard, 1985), 24.
4. Jeanne Giovannoni and Rosina M. Becessa, *Defining Child Abuse* (New York: Free Press, 1979), 14.
5. Carl, *Child Abuse,* 24.
6. Ray E. Helfer and Henry C. Kempe, *The Battered Child Syndrome* (Chicago: University of Chicago Press, 1968).
7. I divided two thousand deaths per year into 8736 hours (per year). This figures out to be 4.368 hours per death.

CHAPTER 2

1. Maria Roy, *Children in the Crossfire* (Deerfield Beach, Fla.: Health Communications Inc., 1968), 87–88.
2. James J. Mead and Glenn M. Balch, Jr., *Child Abuse and the Church: A New Mission* (Costa Mesa, Calif.: HDL Publishing, 1987), 53.
3. Statistics provided by the National Committee for the Prevention of Child Abuse and the U.S. Department of Justice.

CHAPTER 7

1. Adele Mayer, *Sexual Abuse: Causes, Consequences, and Treatment of Incestuous and Pedophilic Acts* (Holmes Beach, Calif.: Learning Publications, 1985), 6.
2. Linda Tschirhart Sanford, *The Silent Children: A Parent's Guide to the Prevention of Child Sexual Abuse* (New York: McGraw-Hill, 1982), 154.
3. Mayer, *Sexual Abuse,* 7.
4. Jacqueline Blais and Carolyn Pesce, "Rape Called Enormous Problem," *USA Today,* 23 April 1992, 6A.
5. Dayan Edwards and Eliana Gil, *Breaking the Cycle: Assessment and*

Treatment of Child Abuse (Los Angeles: Cambridge Graduate School of Psychology, 1986), 91.

6. Ibid.

7. Flora Colao and Tamar Hosansky, *Your Child Should Know* (New York: Berkley, 1985), 51.

8. Edwards and Gil, *Breaking the Cycle,* 96.

9. Mayer, *Sexual Abuse,* 8.

10. Lynn Heitritter and Jeanette Vought, *Helping Victims of Sexual Abuse* (Minneapolis: Bethany, 1989), 91.

11. Susanne Sgroi, *Handbook of Clinical Intervention in Sexual Abuse* (Lexington, Mass.: D.C. Heath, 1982), 218.

12. Edwards and Gil, *Breaking the Cycle,* 96.

13. Mark Mayfield, "Man Convicted in N.C. Child Sex Abuse Case," *USA Today,* 23 April 1992, 6A.

14. Kenneth V. Lanning, "Child Protection Alert," *FBI Law Enforcement Bulletin* (January 1984), 10.

15. A. N. Groth and C. M. Loredo, "Juvenile Sexual Offenders: Guidelines for Assessment," *International Journal of Offender Therapy and Comparative Criminology* 25, no. 3 (1983): 31–39.

16. Michael O'Brien and Walter Bera, "Adolescent Sexual Offenders: A Descriptive Typology," *Preventing Sexual Abuse* 1, no. 3 (fall 1986): 1.

17. Heitritter and Vought, *Helping Victims of Sexual Abuse,* 92.

18. Edwards and Gil, *Breaking the Cycle,* 92–95.

19. Ibid., 98.

CHAPTER 9

1. Statistics provided by the National Committee for the Prevention of Child Abuse.

2. R. J. Gelles, "Child Abuse As Psychopathology: A Sociological Critique and Reformulation," *American Journal of Orthopsychiatry* 43 (July 1973): 620–21.

3. James J. Mead and Glenn M. Balch, Jr., *Child Abuse and the Church: A New Mission* (Costa Mesa, Calif.: HDL Publishing, 1987), 35.

4. Dayan Edwards and Eliana Gil, *Breaking the Cycle: Assessment and Treatment of Child Abuse* (Los Angeles: Cambridge Graduate School of Psychology, 1986), 34.

5. Ibid., 33.

6. R. W. Gould and M. G. Morris, *The Neglected and Battered Child Syndrome: Role Reversal in Parents* (New York: Child Welfare League of America, 1963).

7. E. H. Clark and J. J. Tracy, "Treatment for Child Abusers," *Social Work* 19 (May 1974): 339.

8. Angela R. Carl, *Child Abuse! What You Can Do about It* (Cincinnati: Standard, 1986), 20.
9. Mead and Balch, *Child Abuse and the Church,* 35.
10. Edwards and Gil, *Breaking the Cycle,* 40.
11. Ibid.
12. Carl, *Child Abuse,* 21.
13. Vincent DeFrancis, *The Fundamentals of Child Protection* (Englewood, Colo.: The American Humane Association, 1978), 26.
14. Edwards and Gil, *Breaking the Cycle,* 61.
15. Mead and Balch, *Child Abuse and the Church,* 119.
16. Ibid., 19–21.
17. Edwards and Gil, *Breaking the Cycle,* 76.
18. Ibid.

APPENDIX A

1. Dr. Dobbins's comments are taken from his video course, *Caring for the Family of God:* "Facing the Issues of the '90s" (volume 2), in which he discusses child sexual abuse. EMERGE Ministries, Inc., offers mental health ministries in treatment, training, and prevention.

Anderson, B. *When Child Abuse Comes to Church* (Minneapolis: Bethany, 1992). This 174-page paperback is written from a pastor's heart. It includes the chapters "How to Deal with the Media," "Roadblocks to Healing," and "Prevention."

Delaplane, David. *Victims: Manual for Clergy and Congregation* (Washington, D.C.: National Victim Resource Center, 1993). A guide for clergy and religious leaders on responding to the needs of victims of crime.

Gil, Eliana. *Outgrowing the Pain* (New York: Dell, 1983). This eighty-eight-page paperback provides a concise overview of victims' feelings, experiences, and reactions in response to abuse in their past. It is recommended to help victims and to help their friends and family better understand some of what those who have been abused feel, think, and act out.

Hammar, Richard, Steven Klipowicz, and James Cobble, Jr. *Reducing the Risk of Child Sexual Abuse in Your Church* (Matthews, N.C.: Christian Ministry Resources, 1993). Complete and practical guidebook for prevention and risk reduction. Includes a major section on policy formation for churches.

Johnson, Becca Cowan and For Kids' Sake, Inc. *For Their Sake: Recognizing and Responding to Child Abuse* (American Camping Association, 1992). This 204-page paperback is designed to assist camp directors and staff, youth ministry leaders, teachers and principals, and child-care providers. She writes the book from her vast knowledge of education and camping.

Mead, James J., Glenn Balch, and Elizabeth Maggio. *Investigating Child Abuse* (Chino, Calif.: R. C. Law & Co., 1992). This excellent resource deals with investigating the issues that surround child abuse. Contains extensive bibliography for each chapter.

Sanford, Doris. Hurts of Childhood and In Our Neighborhood series. Excellent series of books written for children who have experienced trauma and pain. Topics include molestation, foster care, adoption, alcoholism, AIDS, and death. Write to Doris Sanford, Heart to Heart Inc., 2115 S.E. Adams, Milwaukie, OR 97222-7773; or phone (503) 654-3870.

ABOUT THE AUTHORS

Wayne and Diane Tesch, Founders
of Royal Family Kids' Camps

For eighteen years Wayne and Diane Tesch served on
the staff of Newport-Mesa Christian Center in Costa Mesa,
California, where Wayne was the senior associate pastor.
Their ministry brought hundreds of people through their
home as new programs and ministries were formed and nur-
tured. These ministries included dual-career workshops,
engaged-couples seminars, adult-leadership training, day
camps, resident camps, and in 1985 a camp designed for
abused and neglected children.

Wayne's gifts as a visionary, encourager, trainer, and mentor combined with Diane's administrative skills and franchise-
training background to form a dynamic husband-wife team
to launch and establish Royal Family Kids' Camps, Inc., a
full-time, nationwide ministry to abused and neglected children.

The love and compassion Wayne and Diane Tesch feel for
children has always drawn them to meeting the needs of kids
in both their church and the community. In 1990 Royal Family Kids' Camps, Inc. was designed to meet the unique and
unusual needs of abused and neglected children, giving them
hope and an assurance that there are loving adults who care
deeply about them. The weeklong summer camps have
received enthusiastic response and endorsement from the

county social-service agencies whose subjects have benefited from their camping program.

Currently, Wayne and Diane travel across America on behalf of Royal Family Kids' Camps, Inc., seeking to mobilize two hundred churches that will commit one week each summer to sponsor a camp for abused and neglected children in the local church community, duplicating the training model first established in Southern California.

Wayne Tesch is a member of the Child Abuse Council of Orange County. He has been appointed to serve on the eight-member advisory board to clergy for the California Consortium for Prevention of Child Abuse, a state-funded agency.

The Tesches reside in Southern California and may be contacted at Royal Family Kids' Camps, Inc., 1068 Salinas Avenue, Costa Mesa, CA 92626, or by calling (714) 548-6828.

PUTTING THE PIECES TOGETHER:
Royal Family Kids' Camps, Inc. video

I would like a copy of the Royal Family Kids' Camps explanatory video, *Putting the Pieces Together*. Please use my donation to continue expanding Royal Family Kids' Camps and helping the abused and neglected children of America find hope and healing. I have enclosed a gift of:

☐ $25 ☐ $50 ☐ $100 ☐ $____

NAME:_____

ADDRESS:_____

CITY:_____ STATE: _____ ZIP:_____

Please send your gift today:

Royal Family Kids' Camps
1068 Salinas Avenue
Costa Mesa, CA 92626

Thank you for your love and generosity. Royal Family Kids' Camps is a nonprofit organization. IRS regulations allow you to deduct the portion of your gift over the cost of the video; you will be sent a receipt for that amount.

How Did *You* Survive?

If you were abused as a child, you may have been shaped by a person or program that helped you overcome the scars of your past. Please share your story in writing with Wayne and Diane Tesch for possible inclusion in an upcoming book. Fill out the coupon below, and include the name, address, and phone number of a pastor, teacher, or adult friend who can verify your story. Thank you, and may God continue to guide you on the road to healing and spiritual health.

YOUR NAME _____

ADDRESS _____

CITY, STATE, ZIP _____

PHONE (___) ___-____

BIRTHDAY __/__/__   ☐ Male ☐ Female

NAME OF REFERENCE _____

ADDRESS _____

CITY, STATE, ZIP _____

PHONE (___) ___-____

RELATIONSHIP TO YOU _____

Please type or print your story and the key elements of success in overcoming the long-lasting effects of child abuse, and return the document with this coupon to:

Royal Family Kids' Camps
1068 Salinas Avenue
Costa Mesa, CA 92626